2 WEEK LOAN

This item is to be returned to the library on or before the last date stamped below.

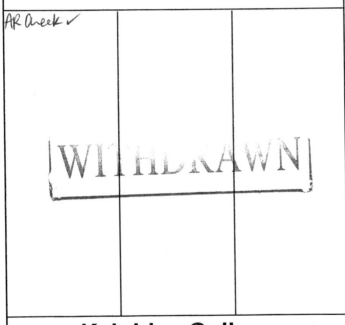

AR Week ✓

WITHDRAWN

Keighley College

To renew telephone 01535 685010

library@leedscitycollege.ac.uk

FATHERHOOD

FATHERHOOD

EDITED BY SEAN FRENCH

Published by VIRAGO PRESS Limited, 1992
20–23 Mandela Street, Camden Town, London NW1 0HQ

This collection copyright © Sean French, 1992
Introduction copyright © Sean French, 1992
Copyright © in each contribution held by the author, 1992

Grateful acknowledgement is made to John Agard c/o Caroline Sheldon
Literary Agency, for kind permission to use 'For My Daughter Yansan
Yashoda' from *Mangoes and Bullets*, published by Pluto Press (1985); to Faber
and Faber for kind permission to use the extract from 'A Man Meets a Woman
in the Street' from *The Complete Poems of Randall Jarrell*, published by
Faber & Faber (1971); to Ben Ulenga for kind permission to use the extract
from his poem 'Fathers'.

The right of Sean French to be identified as the editor of this work has been
asserted by him in accordance with the Copyright, Designs and Patents Act,
1988

A CIP catalogue record for this book is available from the British Library

Printed in Britain by Bookcraft (Bath) Ltd.

CONTENTS

To Edgar, Anna and Hadley

INTRODUCTION

SEAN FRENCH

A s I was preparing to write this, I received, quite by chance, copies of documents which a relative had sent to my father. Birth and marriage certificates and some data from the national census of 1851 trace my family over the three generations from my grandfather to his great-grandfather. By my family, I mean, of course, only the name of French, as if the name somehow traced the main river of my inheritance, from which names like Neale, Helliwell and Wakefield branch off irrelevantly. All the names on these forms are insubstantial, ghostly presences yet the women exist at another remove, shadows of shadows. The forms I have before me are themselves copies, but they do testify to an original in an archive somewhere that was signed by my great-great-great-grandfather and my great-great-grandfather. The forms also report that my great-great-great-grandmother, Johannah Neale, and my great-great-grandmother, Mary Helliwell, signed the birth certificates of their children not with their names but with a cross.

The branch of my family constituted by my great-grandmother, Emma French, *née* Wakefield, is doubly truncated, since her marriage certificate informs me that her father's name was Frank Miner. Here at least I will be maintaining a family tradition. When my partner was pregnant we decided that a girl – and subsequent siblings – would take her surname, a boy would take mine. My daughter now has French between her second and fourth names, like an old photograph stowed in an inaccessible cupboard.

I already knew that I knew very little about my family history, paternal or otherwise. I now see that the problem was not with what I didn't know, but with what I did know that wasn't so. I knew that my father's family were Irish immigrants who had moved to Liverpool to work as labourers on the canal. To my grandparents' fury and shame, my mother christened me in commemoration of the Irish forebears from whom they had struggled so effectively to escape. Not only had I inherited nothing from my grandfather but I did not even know his first name until my uncle named his youngest son Robin after him.

Such was my sense of family tradition and it was entirely false. John French, whose daughter, Margaret, was born in Ireland in 1847 and whose youngest son, John, was born in Liverpool in 1849, was classified as a tailor. The family was then, it seems, downwardly mobile, for the younger John classified himself as a labourer when he registered the birth of his own son in 1876. And when that son was married in 1898, he and his father-in-law were both labourers as well.

Names are generally an instrument in the invention of tradition. At the porter's lodge of the ridiculous undergraduate institution I attended, I frequently used to be asked, when giving my name, if it was spelt with two small 'f's. It was satisfying to learn a year or two later in a palaeography course that the name ffrench, like so many ancient traditions, is a nineteenth-century affectation. Victorians would consult an old document and then adopt what they supposed to be the original spelling of their name, unaware that a doubled 'f' was simply another way of representing a capital letter.

My family was safe from this particular absurdity because there were no old family documents to consult, but we have managed to create a couple of our own. I was always surprised at my grandfather having been christened Robin, a name that sounds about as likely for a nineteenth-century Liverpool labourer as Evelyn or Tarquin. The records show that he was in fact called Robert.

Then there is my own name, which was originally my middle name, Julian having to be abandoned when the unfortunate coincidence was pointed out that the ill-fated hero of one of my father's favourite novels, John O'Hara's *Appointment in Samara*, was called Julian English. I like the name Sean. It's quick to write, classless and cannot be irritatingly shortened. But it is like a neo-Georgian portico added to a Victorian building as part of an ignorant piece of restoration. We were a Protestant Irish family and the documents I have do not show a single overtly Irish first name. My youngest brother was named Karl in acknowledgement of the 50 per cent of his genes that were transported to England from Sweden in 1958; my brother Patrick and I were named in misplaced tribute to the roughly 3 per cent of our inheritance that arrived in Liverpool in about 1848.

My foremothers had one advantage over the men whose names they took. They were certain that they were the mothers of their children, but their husbands or lovers could never be entirely sure of their own relation. This insecurity was articulated by Dr Johnson in a conversation recorded in James Boswell's *Life*:

'I mentioned to him a dispute between a friend of mine and his lady, concerning conjugal infidelity, which my friend had maintained was by no means so bad in the husband, as in the wife. JOHNSON. "Your friend was in the right, Sir. Between a man and his Maker it is a different question: but between a man and his wife, a husband's infidelity is nothing. They are connected by children, by fortune, by serious considerations of community. Wise married women don't trouble themselves about infidelity in their husbands." BOSWELL. "To be sure there is a great difference between the offence of infidelity in a man and that of his wife." JOHNSON. "The difference is boundless. The man imposes no bastards upon his wife."'

The traditional British marriage can be seen as a bargain proceeding from this anxiety about paternity. If the woman had relinquished her name and all her possessions, and depended on her husband for her basic subsistence, then it was in her interest to convince him that her children were also his. In a culture where all that matters is the passing on of genes, this certainty need not be crucial, since men might act like certain breeds of monkey and conclude that their best strategy was to impregnate as many females as possible. (One has only to read the works of Norman Mailer to realise that this still has its advocates.) But in a society based on the ownership of property, people need to feel sure they are leaving it to their authentic descendants. This is why the *droit de seigneur* could only exist in a feudal society, symbolising as it did the fact that male serfs had no property to leave and thus no need to be sure of whether their children were their own. In fact, if they all *were* sure of their paternity, their desire to obtain property to leave them might become irresistible. It didn't matter how much Lorenzo da Ponte bowdlerised Beaumarchais's *Le Mariage de Figaro* when preparing the libretto for Mozart. From the central situation that survives, of Figaro denying the Count possession of his wife's body, everything else follows.

Our view of property, marriage and sexual morality is now hopelessly muddled but the paternal anxiety survives. It's not just that the New Man might be reluctant to demonstrate his sensitivity by getting back from work in order to read a story to a child that he thinks may not be his. It is my experience of a year of fatherhood that people are more insistent in pointing out the resemblance of the baby to the father than to the mother, as if each such observation were a testimonial of authenticity. This is scarcely a scientific finding, but even if it is not strictly true, it doesn't matter, since my perception of the supposed phenomenon must itself be a demonstration that the anxiety exists. But then perhaps I have a special reason to be anxious, or perhaps people are being overly insistent about the resemblance because they know something I don't about reasons there may be to doubt my actual paternity. Excuse me, if I stop writing for a few minutes while I go and look at my daughter.

Well, that's all right. It's not just that she obviously looks like me, but on that flap of flesh that protects the ear, the one that you press into the cavity when you try to block out sound (Nicholson Baker would know what it's called), well, I have a small lump on my right one and my daughter has a small lump on her left one, so the chances must be millions and millions to one that we are not related, unless, that is we both have small tumours on our ears, but even that would be more likely if we really were father and daughter, wouldn't it?

I suspect that most men are uneasy with the idea of fatherhood in a way that women are not with motherhood. Most men become fathers twice. The first occasion is at the moment of conception. After my daughter had been conceived I could have absconded, been kidnapped by aliens, died, and she would have been born just the same. And those men who do depart for one reason or another are still fathers in a sense that the best stepfather in the world will never be. Yet when the baby is born the man has to become a father in a different, public way, putting on the old robes, creaky, ill-fitting, moth-eaten, worn with overuse. As the reader of this book will see, this second fatherhood is a contract that has to be renegotiated every time. If the first paternal anxiety is about the questionable male relationship to the baby, then the second is an envy of the mother's unquestionable relationship. One of the most potent myths ever invented by a woman is Mary Shelley's Frankenstein, the man harnessing all technology in order to cobble together his own baby with lightning and scraps from the graveyard.

I grew up on another, more insidious version of that myth, Dr Seuss's story for children, *Horton Hatches the Egg*. Readers may recall that Maisie the lazy bird is tired of sitting on her egg in the jungle and she departs on holiday, enlisting Horton, a passing elephant, to sit on it for her. Horton faces terrible hardships. He is rained and snowed upon, then captured and displayed in a circus to mocking audiences, but he keeps his promise: 'I meant what I said, and I said what I meant / An elephant's faithful one hundred per cent.' Just as the egg is about to hatch, Maisie returns to claim her egg, but then it hatches and out pops a little elephant with wings. Thirty years *avant la lettre* is this not the dream of the New Man, that by being sensitive enough, by finding the womanly side of himself, the woman can be supplanted altogether? The climax of this tendency was enacted in Tariq Ali's 1991 novel, significantly entitled *Redemption*, in which, when the mother fails to produce milk for the baby, it is miraculously suckled by its father.

Anxiety is a form of aggression, and if fathers envy the mother's biological connection, this is accompanied by a sense that motherhood is just a little too easy. The baby pops out and is applied to the breast; what is that compared with the struggles that fathers face? Robert Benton's utterly monstrous film, *Kramer vs. Kramer*, is an epic in which Dustin Hoffman's achievement is not to kill the white whale or forge a mighty sword but to learn how to make breakfast for his son. *Field of Dreams* is another epic in which Kevin Costner, the New Man's answer to Gary Cooper, heals his psyche, and by implication that of America, by summoning his father from beyond the grave in order to throw a baseball with him. The bond between father and child, especially father and son, is portrayed as an exclusion of the mother. In his deranged megalomaniac movie *The Alamo*, in which, as one critic observed, the slogan 'Better Dead than Red' is replaced by the slogan 'Better Tex than Mex', John Wayne/Davy Crockett compares the feeling that the word 'republic' gives him to the feeling a man gets when he holds his first son in his arms. The mother–child relation is introverted, private; the father–child relation is extroverted, public, and public-spirited.

This anthology of essays on fatherhood is necessarily an unrepresentative failure. Major varieties of the species are entirely absent. There is, for example, that substantial minority of men who don't even know they are fathers. I don't know any actual examples of this class but I do know a man who doesn't know that he was the father of a foetus that was aborted. I didn't approach him for a contribution. There is no spokesman in these pages on behalf of the sexually abusing fathers that figured so prominently in the accounts of Freud's female patients that he concluded that this demonstrated they didn't exist. (It's as if a policeman were to protest to a complainant: 'I'm sorry but I'm going to need a lot less evidence than *that*, if you expect me to believe such a fantastic story.')

We know from the crime statistics that many fathers hate their own fathers and hate their children. I would like to have had the views of the young father who beat his eleven-month-old daughter to death at Christmas 1990 because she was unable to open her presents, but he is currently inaccessible. We know from the statistics on one-parent families that a good many fathers are not able or willing to take on the role in any way at all. The man who, I had hoped, would write from personal experience of this proved in the end unwilling to commit it to paper. I trust that somewhere, in a parallel dimension, there is a shadow version of this book in which his copy did arrive, along with essays by the other potential contributors who turned me down, the public figure and pundit who said he could not write because he felt he had been a failure as a father; the person who said that fatherhood was something she wished to forget about.

In those other dimensions there are also copies of this book appearing identical in every way to the one you are holding, except for the title. My original thought was *Fatherland* which seemed to me very Virago, with its suggestion of patriarchal totalitarianism, but this was considered too grim and, besides, a thriller of that title appeared earlier this year. My next idea was *From Here to Paternity* which was considered not grim enough, sounding more like a collection of articles from *Punch* on the 'funny side of fatherhood, an irreverent sideways look at the world of changing nappies and escaping to the 19th hole'. In the end a simple title seemed best. As Dr Johnson defined 'fatherhood' in his *Dictionary*: 'The character of a father; the authority of a father'. But then, Dr Johnson was childless.

FATHERHOOD, FROM THE GERMAN

LES MURRAY

> *Becoming a father, that is no*
> *Achievement. Being one is, though.*

FOR MY DAUGHTER
YANSAN YASHODA

JOHN AGARD

at two minutes past six
you screamed your wombsong coming
into a new world
of shape and sound

what brings you to these shores little one?
what dreams lie curled
in this your feathersoft fist
she who mothered you can never tell

what pains will touch your path
between the cradle and the grave
no one knows

but like the flower that grows
knowing not which wind
will one day uncomb its bloom
so must you my child

so sleep well little one
and dream your dream
before the price of sleep becomes too dear

THE EXTENDED FATHER

ALAN BRIEN

When making generalisations, it is always wise to be specific. So far as I speak at all for my generation on fatherhood, I must fence around my assertions with the caveat that these will tend to be those of a working-class intellectual of sorts, born in the North during what we still call *the* slump, on active service (in my instance a flight sergeant airgunner) in what we still call the Last War, educated at grammar school and university (Oxford), married young (twenty-one in 1947) and soon on the make in some challenging, moderately lucrative, vaguely creative occupation (Fleet Street). There and then, among such, over the next fifteen years after the age of eighteen, I can confidently claim that I never met another man who positively wanted to be a father.

Of course, almost all of my old-home-towners, wartime comrades, fellow students, drinking companions, upwardly striving, over-achieving by-liners and telly faces, admen and back-benchers, actors and authors, naturally aspired to sire a child some time, eventually. They were only waiting for the right job, the right state of the market, the right international situation, the right house, possibly the right spouse – for this was the first generation of our sort to begin to accept divorce as commonplace. A reasonable option and a valid extra choice, the 'second act' Scott Fitzgerald mourned as deleted from ordinary American lives, formerly available as serial polygamy only to Woolworth heiresses and Hollywood stars. We were discovering there was no rule confining us for life to one wife, one set of in-laws, one family. Why, there was a Fleet Street columnist, on the *Sunday Telegraph* of all papers, who had been married five times.

With such a variety of potential gene pools to fish in, so many opportunities for profitable nepotism and exciting semi-incest being offered by marriage and remarriage, why should we imprison ourselves within the safe monotony of the nuclear family, content with offspring who can aspire to be little more than, as Paine described the typical English aristocrat, 'the tenth inheritor of a foolish face?' It seemed our duty to research the physical and mental capabilities of as many potential mothers of our children as were pleasurably available. But the more I assured everyone that I could not wait to become a father – my mother, my mother-in-law, my old headmaster's wife, my pals, my wife, even myself – the more excuses I found to postpone pregnancy. The H-bomb was among the most convincing. How could any woman even think for a moment of bringing into this soon to be vaporised planet an innocent creature who would almost certainly never reach maturity?

As well as being convenient, these fears were also genuine and disturbing. I knew at least half a dozen quite close contemporaries whose development remained arrested in the caterpillar stage through a conviction that none of us would survive the terminal decade of the fifties in this world's existence. Not only did they reject parenthood and marriage, they refused to consider taking out a mortgage or life insurance, joining the staff of any firm, becoming members of any club or party, even investing in more than one suit and a couple of shirts, bothering to have a bank account or an entry in the telephone directory.

A few carried their distrust of the future, doubting indeed that it would ever exist, so far as to never make any appointments of any kind, even for a drink, more than a week ahead. I met one such survivor the other day, pension-less and childless, with no freehold to have enriched him through the property booms, still in the same north London flat, possibly the same suit. He might have been an object of pity and concern if the latest volume of his autobiography had not been selling so well – the craftily inflated tale of a dodgy life, he pointed out, that would not have been worth recounting if he had settled down, as he was so often urged, to marry the boss's daughter, and pass along the family business to their children. I did not like to point out that the firm he refused to take over from the father of his first rich, besotted love had gone bust only a few years later or that I had been air-brushed in his pages out of some of my own favourite anecdotes about me.

But even more than the war that was inevitably to come soon, my generation's attitude to fatherhood was coloured by the war that had just ended. We felt our lost years in the forces as a personal, particular deprivation, a second injustice if, like me, you had grown up accustomed to unemployment, cold and occasionally hunger. The world owed us a loving, if not a living. When we married early, as we mostly did, we looked forward to an ever-extended honeymoon, just the two of us, with no cuckoo in the nest. Marriage was like a passport to a rerun adolescence, only with all the facilities teenagers lacked then – your own bedroom instead of the front-room sofa; an income instead of pocket money; food, drink, entertainment, clothes that pleased you, not your mother. You did not have to be a selfish narcissist to feel that a child would spoil all that, just when you seemed to be making up for rationing, uniforms, regulations, barrack rooms. Fatherhood would be an end to our dream of staying up all night and sleeping late; holidays in remote, dangerous places where you could walk for days in the mountains; flats designed for modern, young people, with plenty of glass walls, steps inside and out, balconies, basements, but no space for the pram in the hall and the washing on the line, in the inner-city, purpose-built block. Whatever that purpose was, it was not fathering a tribe. When these couples woke in the night, it was not to feed the baby.

When our generation pushed on into its own in the mid-fifties – I was then TV critic of the *Observer*, film critic of the *Standard*, and thought there could hardly be any other worlds to conquer – a few of us had already succumbed, not always knowingly, to the lure of fatherhood. At the actual moment of my initiation, I had not become any kind of success, indeed might be described as a spectacular, exemplary failure. I was fired from my job as editor of an obscure 16mm film magazine in Soho two days before my wife gave birth to twins. Surely an omen of epic achievements to come.

The immediate results were not reassuring. A friend on the *Spectator*, whom I'd bullied into commissioning a piece about a new father signing on at the Labour Exchange, called round with the bad news. The editor, Wilson Harris, had turned it down because '*nobody* today is on the dole'. The other mothers in the ward seemed to agree with him. My wife told me their favourite explanation of how I was able to spend most of the day visiting was that I must be a bandleader. Fairly soon I was gainfully employed again, though always as a freelance, nevermore on any employer's staff, entitled to a pension, paid holidays, sick leave, staff car, mileage allowances, redundancy, et cetera. Being a young father, and a multiple parent at one birth, sensitised me to the cost of the hierarchy imposed by the extending family on individuals of equal talent and enterprise.

Those of us who became parents in our twenties were quickly accustomed to being regarded by our bachelor friends, even more so by childless working couples, as handicapped, indigent, rather feckless over-breeders, who were unlikely to reach the top of our profession. And it was true, fatherhood was an expensive indulgence, hobby, perversion, duty or whatever. Simply having to crowd the house with an au pair (in those early days often written, and interpreted, as *au père*) operated like an extra, unfair, discriminatory tax on the philoprogenitive, adding 25 per cent to every outing, weekend, holiday, visit to the theatre or cinema. The babysitter alone, I estimated once, probably cost as much to me as Jeeves did to Wooster – at least Bertie did not have to send him home in a taxi.

But there is one feeling of dread, greater than all of these, a deep revulsion rarely admitted, that impels many of these men I am writing about to reject all urgings towards fatherhood. It may sound frivolous but I am convinced that far more than selfishness or greed, the threat of lack of freedom or the loss of privacy, what scares off these big, tough, manly men is the fear of the well-filled nappy, the stained sheet drying on the radiator.

There seems to be something about that cheesy, beany, cassoulet smell of the infant shit, the ammoniac whiff of infant piss somewhere between a very sour white wine and a concentrated paint stripper, that is too overwhelmingly intimate for the virgin nose of the pre-paternal male. Some fathers never get over this and make sure they will remain forever a stranger to the slopping potty, the warm rubber blanket, the caked sick down the back of the jacket. But these are usually the same ones who never learn to cook or work the washing machine. When they do marry and have children, you wonder why such types should have taken such an unwelcome, unnatural step and then cut themselves off from the whole feminine, childlike, domestic side of cohabitation, the world of emotions, gossip, jokes, confessions, games and ceremonies, so that the wife buys every Christmas and birthday present for all of his and her family, including herself and his secretary, meanwhile writing all the duty letters as well, even to his parents.

The most extreme version of such a relationship was a man I knew who ran off with the woman next door, wife of his best friend, divorced and remarried, but to keep his mother happy somehow persuaded his first wife to pretend the two were still happily together by returning arm in arm with her, twice a year, for family reunions.

I was already a New Man in my first marriage, even before I had heard of the New Woman, not entirely, though I must admit largely, by accident. Intellectually, like many of my generation, I was an adolescent feminist as well as socialist. It was not lost on me that males could win extreme gratitude from females for quite small concessions to equality in our male-dominated, manual workers' world. (I remember the first thing the wives of Communist Party activists would say with awe after a visit from Harry Pollitt, the General Secretary – 'He insisted on doing the washing up!') But respecting principles in the abstract, and recognising the chance to carry them out in life, are notoriously different things. When my wife became pregnant, the second thing I felt was a spontaneous gush of pleasure and pride, even though it was not planned, by me anyway, and I had not been consulted. The first thing was the thought – 'I must tell her I am not up to wiping babies' bottoms.'

As it turned out, she was feeding the twins round the clock, each alternating breast and bottle, and I was on the dole, so even the most macho husband could hardly justify leaving it all to her as 'women's work'. I soon learned that wiping your own babies' bottoms was as an act aesthetically neutral and even, like any job well done – cleaning your teeth, cutting your nails – mildly satisfying.

We Little Fathers, petty pashas and premature patriarchs, felt our isolation all the more keenly as the era of 'swinging London' dawned. While we became gradually exiled to the suburbs, where the bigger, cheaper houses, the better schools, the leafier, safer avenues, were found, spreading out like a bunch of small, county towns, our independent, dependent-less contemporaries prided themselves on cultivating a *Playboy* style in the inner-city villages of the world's fun capital. Neither group was earning exceptionally well, and both used automatically to bump up their status with a little topographical prestidigitation. The family man gave the impression that he was more in Highgate than Crouch End, Hampstead borders rather than Cricklewood proper, while the swingers behaved as if Kentish Town were really upper Soho, or Fulham indistinguishable from the child-free zone of Chelsea. But what we did learn about money was the concept of 'disposable income'. My lot didn't have any, or rather it had already been disposed of, usually before it reached me, on prams, pushchairs, bunk beds, tricycles, cassettes, pop-up books, posters, paddling pools, slides, swings, wellies, capes, and all the other toys 'n' things that fill any middle-class nursery and seem to cost twice the price in the child version that they do in the adult.

Now we all know bachelors and the working couples who also have hangars full of expensive toys. But these are for grown-ups only – cars, music centres, TV projectors, telescopes, satellite dishes, videos, motor boats, helicopters, flats in New York or Paris, cottages in Nantucket or Tuscany – as it becomes clear anything can be a plaything to the young in brain.

My post-1945 generation of young males encountered several firsts in our experience of fatherhood. We had grown up assuming, as lovers had done since the dawn of time, that fucking and fathering were almost inevitably interlinked by nature. When we escaped that tender trap, we usually felt our best contraceptive had been luck. Otherwise we relied on unreliable pelvic tricks generally known as *coitus interruptus* and suiting that term in more ways than one. (Coitus once interrupted, the girl's comment rarely varied – 'Was that it?' she would ask.) There was, of course, also the French letter, awkward, untrustworthy, difficult to obtain without embarrassment, literally unmentionable, even its name a mystery. (How many, if any, except a pedant like me, appreciate its etymology – nothing to do with literature, a 'letter' is an obstacle, as in 'let or hindrance'.) We dreaded above all the girlfriend with child because it meant, not shame, but premature respectability, an early marriage. Once what should have happened, hadn't happened, the chances were what shouldn't have happened, had happened. No wonder it was difficult for us to reject that conditioned response when we were already married, persuading ourselves bad news had become transformed into good news, after a visit to the Register Office.

Parenthood also becomes increasingly complex and difficult as the generations crowd together. Friends in their late fifties – early sixties, still active earners with career prospects unexplored, complain frequently: 'Fifteen years, as parents, looking after the children. And now, another fifteen years, looking after father and mother, as children. Thirty years gone! What happened to the time we were going to set aside for ourselves?'

Fatherhood is a two-way process. But, like looking through a telescope, much depends on which end you use. My father was one of twelve children. He may have had to queue for his turn, but when he turned his eye towards his father he saw a magnified, dazzling, single sun. His father surveyed them all minified, a dozen, small, wayward, barely distinguishable planets. Fatherhood, except for the only child, is not an equal-opportunity activity. My father had four sons and one daughter. I have four daughters and one son. I think we both got the distribution of sexes as we would have ordered them if we could.

My father was a success as a father, and as a husband, though, in strict worldly terms, never achieving higher rank than fully qualified, wage-earning artisan, fitter and turner on the Sunderland Municipal Tramways. He was an Irishman and a socialist, dedicated wheel-horse of the Amalgamated Engineering Union and the Independent Order of Oddfellows, on whose behalf he spent usually three evenings a week quartering the town on bus, trolley-bus and tram, distributing benefits and pensions to the sick, disabled, widows and orphans.

In my teens, if I ever wanted to see him for an hour or so I had to accompany him on his wearisome outings, often made at once both boring and dangerous in the early years of the war by the enveloping blackout, the North Sea winters and the German bombers. I understood then why, wherever I went with my grammar-school mates under cover of the dark and the bombs, to dockside pubs and dubious boarding houses, communist cells and black-market parties, or in the gusty, chill sunlight around street markets and shipyards, along the frothing seafront, across mirrored, tide-evacuated sands, there was sure to be *someone* who asked my name, checking a resemblance, and probing – 'Then you must be Ned's boy?' Sometimes it seemed intrusive and excessive, in a shipbuilding sea port of getting on for a quarter of a million inhabitants. But mostly I was gratified, and flattered on his behalf. So perhaps it was true, as he so often assured us, he was indispensable both at work and in the workers' movement? Certainly he was paid a curious kind of respect by bosses and men, which I recognised because I inherited, during his life, the backwash of it. When things went wrong at the depot, or even in the head office, it was routine for a van to arrive outside our council house, quite late at night

17

or over the weekend, and a workman tell my mother, 'The tramshed foreman is sorry to ask, Mrs Ned, but can we have your man?' Usually it was some manual, technical problem I would expect my father – a wonderfully dextrous operator with his fingers, able to tickle into life strange engines of cranes, generators and pumps he had never seen before – to be able to solve.

But there were other occasions when the General Manager's car came with a proper driver, collecting him to give his thoughts on some larger question of strategy or overall change in policy. We never were told any details – 'I was asked for my thoughts and I gave them' – but it is my theory now that he was useful for two things. He was able to give the management the most accurate reflection of the feelings of the men available, and he could also add a viewpoint that today would be categorised as 'lateral thinking'. We were used to his gnomic mottoes and tended to underrate them. Outsiders were more impressed and I wish I had paid more attention to the bits of parental wisdom he dispensed as he was dying. I can only recall two – 'Always shout before you're hurt, afterwards it may be too late' and 'Always let the other fella be embarrassed.'

My father's father, 'Black Peter' Brien, had been born in Cork. Once upon a time he was a sea captain, with his own small boat. This reputedly sprang a leak and sank in Sunderland harbour, leaving him as much a castaway as Crusoe, reduced to running a corner shop rather badly. Perhaps this was why my father, for all his apparent ubiquity, retained the demeanour of an outsider in the Geordie heartland though he never seemed to display any of the stereotypes of the Irishman. Indeed, except when suffused with glee at the results of some impish, mischievous trick, he was a stately, impassive six-footer who looked, as one of his closer friends in the tramshed observed, as if he had been 'born with a boil on the back of his neck'.

Such is the power of the parental image, especially living on after the original has vanished, that some primitive urge pushes the children on to idealise and immortalise the dead father or mother. There is nothing he would have hated more – he once claimed to have written to Stalin protesting against the insult to Lenin's principles involved in the exhibition of his mummified corpse. He had many faults, but they were never more than irritating or exasperating. He was stubborn and secretive and a bit vain, rather unnecessarily severe upon those too cowardly to stand up for their rights and spit in their opponent's eye.

He had convictions of his own talents that were never shaken, no matter how many times disproved. But they were all minor flaws, comical as much as painful, and operated at his own expense as well as that of others. For example he was absolutely convinced he had a bump of direction which made it impossible ever to get lost. The result was that on his annual (unpaid) holiday up in the hills of Weardale and Teesdale, we would return to our b. & b. farmhouse around midnight every night, my sister, mother and I, trailing behind a striding explorer convinced that the extra ten miles had been a deviation scarcely worth mentioning.

One quality my father possessed that is an essential of the perfect parent was . . . drama. He was embarrassing, confusing, frightening even, erratic, unpunctual, unconventional, sometimes ludicrous, all the things teenagers find so shaming about those who have brought them into this world. But he was never predictable, never boring, never entirely grown up, and so never safe in the presence of real adults. His maxim about shouting before you're hurt was not metaphorical. He was just about as accident prone as you can be and stay alive. My pulse would beat at any knock on the door (friends let themselves in round the back) at an unusual hour while he was out. Around twice a year my excitement was justified. Half the street would be out watching my father being carried on a door from the back of a lorry and up our front steps. And one of his tramshed entourage would whisper to me that Ned had grasped a live power line, fallen into an inspection pit, backed into a bus, walked through a sheet of glass. None of my middle-class school chums had fathers who lived so dangerously, even in wartime. It was like being the son of a commando or a fighter pilot.

If my father was high among desirable dads, I have to say that for him I had a good rating as a suitable offspring. I was the last born of the five, junior to the nearest sibling, my sister, by six years. My two elder brothers had already joined the RAF in the mid-thirties driven out of Sunderland by the slump and mass unemployment. My next brother, though a pacifist, volunteered for the army the day war broke out. My sister held off for a while then followed into the women's services, the ATS. By the end of 1939 I was the only child at home and, in effect, an only child. The war deepened my father's commitment to the Left. He indoctrinated me, and I politically educated him in return. Together, we listened to Radio Moscow. Though we were all, needless to say, Labour supporters, I was the only other member of the family dedicated to the class struggle in a serious fashion.

This identification with the proletariat mildly surprised my three brothers then, and continues to do so today, since, having been skilled wage earners all their lives, they tend, or pretend, to regard a writer as someone who has never done a real day's work in his life. My father, however, liked to see me selling the banned *Daily Worker*, under one or other of its many false names, at street corners and in pubs. He was also proud when I led a strike, a criminal offence in wartime, of exploited shipyard apprentices abandoned by his own union.

I admired his instinctive egalitarian militancy, whenever he was face to face with the establishment, though often I chickened out when it came to a clash, person to person, the have-not against the haves. A typical situation would be the two of us walking across some wild, unfrequented, but privately owned, moors above Weardale or Teesdale and finding ourselves asked to leave his land by the local laird. My father had a whole act to deal with this. It was all a matter of reason and logic. Of course he would obey the law, though regarding it as iniquitous, but did this gentleman here have about him deeds to prove his title to the land. No? Well, then my father could proclaim his ownership on the same evidence. Oh, the gentleman's people were here for generations. Could we meet a couple to confirm the statement? Oh, we are going back centuries to the era when the family took the land by right of conquest, are we?

'Hold my coat, Alan. This gentleman and I are going to fight each other for this desirable stretch of moor.'

Craven, I would cringe and slink away.

Everyone knows there are many problems to being a one-parent family. Not so much is heard about the difficulties encountered in being, like me, a three-family parent. I am now married for the third time, with three grown-up stepchildren, two m, one f, and have three daughters by my first wife and a daughter and son by my second. I cannot pretend that this making and breaking of marriages, starting and stopping of families, has not inflicted damage on my children. I have to admit also that these changes were made by me for my own gratification and that I put my own feelings before those of my offspring. I suspect that the damage done to the unit of parents and children by one of the spouses wishing always to be elsewhere with someone else, though great, may not be as wounding as the damage done to children who think *they* are the ones rejected and unloved. But I did it my way. And I do not think it is self-deceit to feel that the extended many-parented family does bring rewards and pleasures not found in the tight-knit nuclear unit or the one-parent group so long as the adults involved give up being childish and the children are taught what it means to be adult. I know my own daughters have all benefited from being able to talk over their fears and worries and pleasures and hopes about being women with other women who love them but are not too uncomfortably close, flesh of their flesh. I regret that, as a father, I have never been able to supply the one-to-one, conspirators-against-the-world, drama my father gave to me. Rows with racist cab drivers or ignorant head waiters are not quite enough. The best I could do was try to demonstrate to them that, though their father, I am much the same as many other men. I think it is the duty of all parents to demystify, to profane and humanise their role in their children's eyes. It is hard work, not always pleasant but essential if we are ever to accept each other as we ought to be, as soon as possible, as equals.

LEARNING TO BE A FATHER

MERVYN JONES

T he male pursues the female, forces her into a sexually receptive posture, and deposits his seed. The act, unaccompanied by any intimations of affection, is completed within the minimum time rendered possible by the male's ability. The male then departs, turning his mind to other interests. He may never see the female again; he may forget what she looks like; for him, it is one incident among others of the kind. He is aware that she has provided him with satisfaction, but unaware whether he has made her pregnant or not. If he has, she is committed to a gradually developing process of gestation, childbirth and caring for a newly created life. In this process, the male has no necessary part.

Such is the behaviour of males in most animal species, including bulls, stallions, dogs and tom-cats. Such, likewise, is the behaviour of a considerable number of human males in all social cultures – European, American, African or Asian. Biographies tell us of men who, availing themselves of a variety of women, generated dozens or scores of children. The men were monarchs and aristocrats, soldiers and sports-men, writers and artists, religious leaders and gurus, industrialists and newspaper proprietors. All that they have in common is that, in relation to the numerous children, they were fathers in no more than the strictly biological sense.

True, any culture – again, European, American, African or Asian – possesses a broader interpretation of fatherhood. The father is supposed to guarantee food and shelter for the children, watch over their growth, assist them in the acquisition of skills and knowledge. To a greater or lesser extent, most fathers do accept and carry out these responsibilities. The point, however, is that 'being a father' in this praiseworthy sense is optional. It is not inherent in the act of procreation, whereas 'being a mother' is inherent in the act of giving birth. A mother who did not provide an infant with food would be so exceptional as to be designated, by general consent, 'unnatural'. She has become a different person from what she was a year ago before the process of gestation and childbirth began. The father, by contrast, is the same person as a year ago; any change in him (and there may well be no change) is the result of conscious decision.

In other words: a woman does not need to learn how to be a mother. Of course, she may for all sorts of reasons – ignorance, selfishness or the pressure of other duties or wishes – be an inadequate mother; but she knows the essential meaning of the job. A man always needs to learn how to be a father. Many, everywhere, refuse to learn. Many convince themselves that, given the presence of the mother, it is unnecessary. Some try but give up before they have made much progress. For learning to be a father is not easy.

How hard is it? If I say that it is harder than learning to be a street cleaner or an assembly-line worker, anyone would agree that I am stating the obvious. But if I say that it is harder than learning to be an architect or a theatre director, a research physicist or an eye surgeon, most men will protest that I am being ridiculous. After all, there are many more fathers than members of these professions. Yet there is a sense in which this is true. No one can learn to be a father through a course of study, through reading the right books, or even through dedicated practice. One learns (if one does learn) by entering into a new and unpractised form of relationship. Many men, including men of goodwill who would like to succeed and be 'good fathers' or 'real fathers', find this very difficult. Some find it totally impossible.

My own father, Ernest Jones, was a psychoanalyst. On the face of it, he was excellently equipped for learning to be a father. He certainly had no objections to learning, and knew that the process is open ended. In fact, he said that he would like the words 'He died learning' to be engraved on his tombstone. He had spent years in learning, first the profession of medicine, then the new and experimental profession of psychoanalysis. His working hours were spent in building up the special relationship of understanding and trust that is necessary between an analyst and a patient. He had learned, too, how to build up successful relationships with women (various, including my mother). In the world of psychoanalysis, he had to work hard at coming to terms with other analysts from different national and cultural backgrounds whose strong personalities clashed with his own. Thus, human insights and human relationships were his particular line of country. And yet, despite all these qualifications and for that matter achievements, I cannot say that he was ever outstandingly successful in learning to be a father. The truth was – and he was aware of this – he found it difficult. There must have been many simpler and less educated men – bus drivers or shopkeepers, say – who learned it more readily than Ernest Jones.

I might add that time and practice did not make it easier for him. He experienced more conflicts, more misunderstandings and more sheer puzzlement with regard to my younger sister and brother than with me. Admittedly, he had the disadvantage of starting rather late in his own life, becoming a father only when he was over forty. He may, quite simply, have found the renewed task too tiring. It's probably true that most fathers (unlike most mothers) manage better with the older children in the family than with the younger.

I admired my father enormously. He was better at everything than I could ever aspire to be, including his leisure pursuits, which were chess and skating. (He tackled and solved chess problems, and was engaged at any given time in several correspondence games; he served as a judge in skating contests and wrote a book called *The Elements of Figure-Skating*.) I knew, as soon as I could understand anything of the kind, that in his work he was a man of great distinction. Inevitably, all this was somewhat daunting, but I think I can honestly say that I admired my father more than I envied him – presumably because he was so much out of my league that there was no question of competition. Nevertheless, it was just the distinction and achievement of Ernest Jones that prompted a goading, frustrating question: if he was so damn good at everything else, why couldn't he be equally good at being a father?

Then, being the son of a dedicated Freudian was bound to confront me with a particular difficulty. I learned (not from my father, who was averse to talking about professional matters and certainly never sought to indoctrinate me, but from my general reading) of the existence of the Oedipus complex. I don't recall my exact age at the time, but I know that I was seized with panic. Did I really want to kill my father? Did I want to make love with my mother? (The idea held no attractions whatever for me.) I asked my father, attempting to put on an air of detached intellectual curiosity, whether this complex was indeed universal in humankind or whether it admitted of exceptions. He assured me it was an integral part of the human condition, whether in the primeval forest or in the most sophisticated and cultivated environment. To have discovered its universality, he explained, was the mark of Freud's genius. I felt – as the son of a Calvinist preacher might have felt on making acquaintance with the doctrine of original sin – the weight of an inescapable doom. I did not want to hate my father; yet, by failing to hate him, I should be repudiating his creed.

There was a further difficulty: once I knew about the Oedipus complex I was debarred from the kind of disagreement, or straightforward conflict, with my father that was available to other sons. If I was rude to him, if I rejected his advice on any matter, if I forgot (quotation marks here – 'forgot') to buy something he had commissioned me to buy when I passed the shops, I was not simply annoying him – I was exemplifying the Oedipus complex in classic form. In my teens I argued with him a good deal, particularly about politics. I naturally felt that on the merits of the question I was right, and sometimes I was. But I was in a no-win situation (a phrase that, in my youth, hadn't yet been coined) because my argument, being an expression of Oedipal rebellion, could not be judged on its merits. I became more intense and heated, and overstated my case. My father then gave a quiet smile, looked at his watch and departed for his consulting room or his study.

In this relationship my father was above all a figure of authority. (If your father figure is your actual father, it simplifies life and is on the whole desirable, or so I think.) In his world, however, he was not the supreme authority, that position being reserved for Sigmund Freud. It was painful for me to realise that there was someone who could correct or rebuke my father, just as the headmaster of my school could correct or rebuke me. Many years later, I read my father's letters home to my mother from San Cristoforo – the place where, in 1923, the mandarins of psychoanalysis, led by the egregious Otto Rank, convinced Freud that Jones was an unworthy disciple and imposed a humiliating censure on him. When I read these letters, my father was long dead (so was Rank) and I was almost sixty years old. But I felt the same mingling of grief and outraged anger – 'how dare they do this to my father?' – that I might have felt had I been still a boy.

In western culture – and much more emphatically in other cultures – the father of the family is still the embodiment of power and authority in the eyes of children. Of course, the status of women has markedly improved, and your mother may be a managing director, a professor, a judge or perhaps a Cabinet minister. Probably, however, a few more generations must pass before equality of men and women is reflected in psychological consciousness, notably the consciousness of children. I am inclined to think that the most devastating moment in a child's life comes with the recognition – which all must experience, except perhaps the children of the Dalai Lama – that a father's supremacy is not absolute, nor universally admitted. Fathers do, in the real world, fail in their undertakings, lose their jobs, get defeated in elections, and have their novels rejected by publishers. They are forced to accept humiliations at the hands of men – or sometimes women – of greater power. The person who feels these setbacks most woundingly is not the father himself (since he can ascribe them to sheer bad luck, or find enough maturity to recognise his errors and limitations) but the child.

Since saying farewell to my own youth, I have become the father of three children – two daughters and a son – and the grandfather of six. I had the advantage that my wife (like almost all women, as I have said, but to a supreme and abundant degree) was a 'natural' mother with little or nothing to learn. It is not for me to say how well or how poorly I learned to be a father. Indeed, however honestly I might try to answer the question, I should soon be floundering in uncertainty. It was always clear to me, however, that I did need to learn. The old saying that 'the admission of ignorance is the beginning of wisdom' is as true in this context as in any other.

Looking at myself as best I can, I should say that my best quality as a father is a negative one: I take no pleasure in the exercise of power. Of course I like to succeed in what I attempt, and when I am involved in a joint enterprise (for instance, on the staff of a weekly paper) I try to make things happen in the way that I prefer, but the power of command over other people is something that makes no appeal to me, and in fact embarrasses me. (I have applied for editorships, but I see with hindsight that the Board was quite right to turn me down.) I think I can say without self-delusion that I also found power over my children unpleasant and embarrassing. I was impatient for them to grow up and make their own decisions without authority from me. I have sometimes been forcefully struck by the insistence of certain fathers on clinging to this authority and refusing to let their children grow up. I remember an occasion in New York when the sixteen-year-old daughter of the family, who had been told to help in preparing dinner, failed to come home in time. Her father pulled her down over his knee and slapped her. Jeanne, my wife, was horrified and detested the man from then on. There may well have been a kinky aspect to this action, but what was central to it – so Jeanne and I thought – was the assertion of power and the pretence that the girl was still a young child.

Through no virtue of my own, I have been fortunate, for two reasons, in achieving some immunity from this demand for authority. Jeanne was a woman of strong character, always willing to take decisions, and incidentally endowed with practical skills which I lacked (I mean, she mended the fuses and that sort of thing, taking over traditional male prerogatives). The children, therefore, were accustomed to look to her to play a role that, by hallowed custom, generally belongs to the father. Secondly, I am a writer working at home and on my own account, and I have belonged to no hierarchy like the psychoanalytic hierarchy in which my father held a – sometimes fiercely contested – position. The children took it for granted that my life was marked by ups and downs, that my books and articles were sometimes rejected, and that decisions which I was powerless to prevent had to be accepted philosophically. Authority was elsewhere, certainly, but authority was unimportant – even, we agreed, fairly absurd and contemptible. Obviously, since most men (and women) are obliged to work in organisations based on hierarchy, my situation was exceptional and privileged. But I am sure that the identification of fatherhood with authority is the greatest – as it is, also, the commonest – of mistakes. It is (to repeat myself) difficult to learn to be a father; but the first essential is to learn how to be a father without being a master.

There is a paradox in this matter of learning, or not learning, to be a father. Since real fatherhood is not inherent in the procreative act, it seems to follow that the man who fails or refuses to be a father is detached and non-responsible – virtually, perhaps even literally, absent. But the detached father is nevertheless a figure of authority. True, he plays no role in the routine of everyday family life; he scarcely knows, and doubtless does not understand, his children. Even so, his potential power is all the more daunting by reason of its remoteness, and his unexpected appearance is more to be feared than his familiar presence could ever be. Recently I read a novel in which a father, who had deserted the mother years ago and whose whereabouts was unknown, made a sudden return which plunged the family into terror, and at once proceeded to issue commands with a total confidence derived from total ignorance. The novel, clearly based on real experience, was entirely convincing. The man had never learned to be a father, and it was appallingly obvious that he never would.

Let us take heart. This novel had a satirical tone and was in places broadly comic. The non-father, in former times entirely self-satisfied and complacent, is feeling the winds of change. He is ridiculed as much as he is feared, and his numbers are diminishing. Reluctantly, he knows that he will have to learn. But there is still a long, laborious way to go.

ABSENT FATHERS

GABRIEL JOSIPOVICI

MY MOTHER'S

For some reason, perhaps because I am approaching my fiftieth birthday, I find myself thinking about him more and more.

I imagine him standing at a tall window, staring out at the grey Parisian sky, or sitting with his brother on a bench in the Allée des Cygnes, gazing into the river as it flows past. What is going through his mind? Thoughts of his wife and two little girls far away in Egypt? Of his own childhood in an Odessa so distant it seems to belong to another time, another world? Or is his mind as blank as his face, across which flit the shadows of the clouds?

*　*　*

I cannot imagine madness. I know that reality is always different from our imaginings and that what we take for empathy is often only sentimentality and self-deception. Yet something drives me to try to imagine, understand.

I study the family photos and see:

– an elegantly dressed couple, exuding an air of happiness, material ease and innocence (they are so young; though the eyes, hers in particular, also convey that Jewish wariness we have all inherited, no matter how light our spirits). He sits on the arm of a sofa, his top hat in his left hand, resting on his left knee, his arm round her waist, drawing her towards him; she stands, drawn in towards him, in her right hand a bunch of flowers, the blooms pointing downwards, her long white dress forming a pool of light as it seems to flow about her feet: my grandparents on the day of their wedding

– a man in a hat at the wheel of a car whose shining metallic bonnet belies the carriage behind, which seems to belong more to the age of the horse than to that of the machine: my grandfather in one of the first cars to be seen in Egypt

– a man with a small black beard and one gleaming eye staring out at the world (the other is in the shadow of his wide-brimmed black-ribboned hat), sitting with a black dog on a sort of camp-stool between his knees, facing him but twisting its head round towards the camera: my grandfather in his mad Parisian years.

As always, it is difficult to separate the people in the photographs from the aura of the period, from all the other photographs of the time I have seen, in books, in exhibitions, in the family albums of others. The costumes, the props, the lighting, the poses, all serve to ensure the triumph of the horizontal over the vertical, of the sedimentation of the past over the continuities of genealogy and family history.

His father, a Jewish tea-merchant in Odessa, had had in later life to be confined to his house, according to one tradition as the result of insanity brought on by drinking too much tea (but is that likely?), according to another because of a nervous ailment (which in nineteenth-century medical parlance could mean many things, from outright lunacy to mild compulsive disorders).

There were three sons, handsome, intelligent, and very big (much more Russian than Jewish in appearance). Two of them decided to become doctors and went abroad to pursue their medical studies, one to Paris, my grandfather to Berlin. In later life they would frequently argue over the relative merits of the two cities as centres of medical advance.

He returned from Berlin in time to enlist as medical orderly in the Russo-Japanese war of 1904. Wounded, he was invalided home.

Was it there he caught the syphilis which would destroy his life? Or as a student in Berlin? (Again, one family tradition has it that it was not syphilis at all but that famous nervous ailment inherited from his father. But only suspected syphilis could account for the conditions imposed by his future father-in-law.)

He made a rapid recovery and was soon off on his travels once again.

In the course of these he visited Egypt and was enchanted by the little town of Helwan, some miles south of Cairo, whose sulphur springs, he always maintained, made it one of the healthiest spots in the world. (As a child, growing up in Egypt in the late forties and early fifties, I would often cycle out with my mother from Maadi, where we lived, to Helwan, taking the desert road and sometimes making a detour to visit the petrified forest – fragments of giant trunks, solid stone now, lying on the sand. Sometimes we would picnic there by the springs, dipping our feet in the cool water. Today Helwan is a mass of crumbling high tower blocks which house a portion of Cairo's enormous workforce. It is here that the endemic bread riots frequently start. But all that lay in the unimaginable future when my grandfather first set eyes on the town.)

He decided to settle there and open a practice. He met the daughter of an Italian doctor, also a Jew, who had married into an old-established Jewish family from Egypt. Soon they were engaged, but the prospective father-in-law insisted on a year's moratorium, presumably to make sure the young doctor's illness showed no sign of recurring.

The year passed without mishap. They married, and within a year their first child, my aunt, was born. He converted to Islam and changed his name from Alexis to Ali. His practice blossomed, and he was much loved by the local population, for he gave his services free to those who could not afford to pay.

(1989. My aunt, now eighty, meets an old Egyptian lady who, on learning who she is, tells her: my mother was one of your father's patients in Helwan before the First War. Ali and his wife were so beautiful, my mother told me, that people said that when they made love the angels in heaven shed tears.)

The baby was taken in triumph to Odessa, to be shown off to the rest of the family. The young couple, who had bought their wedding furniture from Heal's in London, hired an English governess for their child. Might she give her religious instruction in the Anglican faith? she asked. There is only one God, Ali replied. Let her worship Him in whatever way she wishes.

In 1910 a second child, my mother, was born. But this time there was no trip to the town on the Black Sea. The young doctor, who had always been a bit eccentric, liable to do unexpected and even alarming things, was beginning to cause genuine concern. On the boat, returning from a trip to France, he had assaulted a steward. The authorities summoned his wife to come and collect him at the port, where he was being held.

Other incidents followed. In desperation the young wife wrote to her brother-in-law, now a surgeon in Paris, saying that she could no longer cope with her husband. He must come and take him away. Her father strongly disapproved, feeling that a wife must take responsibility for everything her husband does, and that the fact that the wife in question was his beloved eldest daughter made no difference. The brother-in-law too was highly critical of her attitude, and would in fact never speak to her again. She, however, was adamant: her children must be protected. So he came and took Ali back to Paris with him.

In 1914, a few months before the outbreak of the war, his wife and two little girls came to Paris to visit him. Certified now, and confined to his brother's care, he was nevertheless able to have lunch with them, and even accompanied them back to their hotel. That was the last time they would ever see him.

* * *

Sitting here at my desk in a small town in southern England, separated from him by almost the whole of our dark century, I try to imagine him in his last years in Paris, still, after all, a young man, prodigiously gifted and handsome, his life over. I imagine him staring out of the window of his brother's apartment at the grey Parisian sky. Is he thinking of his children? Is he wondering how their lives will turn out? Who they will marry? What their own children will be like? It is barely ten years since, as a young doctor, he enlisted in that other, local war. In those few years he has fallen ill, recovered, found the land of his dreams, settled, married, converted, started a family, eased the suffering of many, been struck down. What does it mean? he asks his brother, as they sit side by side on a bench in the Allée des Cygnes. What can it all mean?

But perhaps he has not spoken out loud at all. At any rate, his brother does not reply.

A year later he is dead. Five years after that his wife, now remarried and with another child, dies in her turn, the victim of a typhoid epidemic which also nearly carries off her second daughter, my mother.

MINE

In the photos I possess he first appears as a plump, overdressed child with dark eyes, holding a helmet in his left hand and the *tricolour* in his right. There is a sizeable toy cannon behind him and the words 'Vive la France' have been scrawled along the bottom by an unknown hand.

Then, in an abrupt transition, he is a striking young man with a dark, lean face, jet-black hair and large brooding eyes

– in whites on a tennis court

– in long shorts amidst pine trees with a dog on a lead

– at the wheel of a large open car (not too dissimilar, this time, to the cars of today)

– in a bathing suit on the beach with my mother.

I have two memories of him, neither of which may be accurate. In one he stands over my bed or cot and says goodbye – or perhaps he does not say anything, I only have the sense that he is leaving. The other is more detailed. I am out for a walk with him and my mother. We are strolling along a grassy path through a park. We come to a pair of large wrought-iron gates. He puts his hands round two of the vertical bars and pushes. Nothing happens. We'll have to climb over, he says. This is exciting. A chance to show what I am made of. I haul myself up and jump down on the other side. I turn and see him pushing open the gate and laughing as he and my mother pass through. In my anger I bend down and pull up a clump of grass. A blade of grass cuts my fingers.

(Is this connected with the recurring nightmare I have about falling from a high building and grasping a rope to save me? The cord sears my fingers as I try to hold it and I am forced to let go.)

What I have learned about my father:

– how his grandfather came to Egypt via Constantinople

– the oppressive presence in his life of his own father, author, at twenty-two (with his brother-in-law), of a novel set in a romantically medieval Cairo, which had a great vogue in France after the First World War and was even short-listed for the Prix Goncourt the year Proust won it with *A l'Ombre des jeunes filles en fleurs*. (The brothers-in-law fell out after this and each tried to write on his own, but as one had the style and the other the ideas they were never able to repeat their first success)

– how he was made to feel unwanted by his parents, first being left for long periods with aunts and uncles, then sent off to Paris to study

– how, returning to Egypt, he married, at twenty, a woman four years older than himself. With her money they left for France, where they enrolled at the University of Aix-Marseille and settled into a flat in Aix-en-Provence. His doctorate completed, they moved to Vence and bought a house, and became acquainted with the elderly Gide, with René Schickele, the Alsatian writer and friend of Thomas Mann, and with France's leading regional novelist, Jean Giono. There he set out to make his own name as a writer, but the clouds of war were gathering, then burst. I was born on 8 October 1940, the last day on which my parents, both Jews, could have sailed from Europe to the relative safety of their native Egypt.

The marriage failed. My parents separated. Italy fell and the Germans descended on Nice, where my mother and I were now living, to pick up the thousands of Jews who had gathered there in the foolish belief that they would be safe. On the afternoon they were due my mother took me out in my pram along the Promenade. On her return she learned that the German trucks had been filled before they reached our hotel. But they would, of course, be back.

My mother ran across a friend from Vence whose husband was in the Resistance. She was horrified to find her still there. You've got to get away. I don't know where to. Leave it to me.

So she arranged for us to escape to the Massif Central with friends of hers who were already going. It was there that my father came to see us a few months later, there that we took our walk through the park with the wrought-iron gates.

The war came to an end. My mother was able to return with me to Egypt. My parents divorced. My father published a volume of three stories under the title (inspired or pretentious, depending on one's taste) *etrange comme la vie*. A little later the French-language papers in Egypt reported that he was marrying the no-longer-young but still popular film star, Viviane Romance (of whom I would catch a glimpse, many years later, in an English TV documentary about the relations of French artists and entertainers to the German occupiers, waving to the crowds as she and – I think – Fernandel departed by train for a tour of the Reich).

In the summer of 1956 my mother and I were about to leave Egypt for England, where I was to spend a year at school in the hope of gaining a scholarship to an English university. My father, with whom I had been in desultory correspondence, wanted me to spend a week or two with him and his wife in Cannes, where they were now living. But the Suez crisis and the subsequent difficulties made by the Egyptian authorities about granting us exit visas meant that I had just enough time to get to England for the start of the school year. I was not sorry to miss him, I think. I was too taken up mourning the loss of my friends and my whole life in Egypt, and too anxious about the future, to want to face the additional burden of confronting an unknown man who also happened to be my father. And my continuing sense of insecurity, even when I had got the scholarship and gone up to Oxford, made me reluctant to press for any quick reunion.

Through an aunt and cousins of his in London, though, I had news of him. It seemed that his second marriage had also ended in divorce and that he was now living in Rome where he was working as a script-writer for a large film studio.

In 1963 I started teaching at one of the new universities and got married. I wrote to give my father the good news, but the letter was returned with 'not known at this address' written on the envelope. The same thing, it seemed, had happened to letters written by his aunt and cousins.

My wife, in Rome for a brief trip, decided to find out what had happened to him, but she too drew a blank. I realised that I had no strong feelings about finding him and made no further effort to trace him. Occasionally, over the years, I wondered what had happened to him or even if he was dead. But surely then, as next of kin, I would have been informed? But one can never be sure.

Whenever I was in Paris I would look up an old friend of my mother's from Egypt, and she would always greet me with the same words: How funny, only yesterday someone was talking to me about your father. She would tell me to wait, and hurry off to phone, returning several minutes later with a piece of paper in her hand. Yes, she would say, handing it to me, my friend's niece (uncle, cousin, brother-in-law) had dinner in Rome recently with him. Here's his address.

But it was always the same address, the film studio from which my letters had been returned with 'not known at this address' scrawled over them.

Occasionally I would try to write about our reunion. I would imagine myself going to Rome, settling into a hotel and starting to make enquiries. I would finally trace him to a specific address, an anonymous block of flats in one of the suburbs. I would mount guard there, waiting for him to appear. He would come out of the building eventually and walk down the street, without a glance at the café where I would be sitting. I would get up and follow, keeping on his tail as he bought provisions and then went into a bar. Sometimes I would imagine him dapper, well cared for; at others bedraggled, his single suit creased and stained, his shoes almost worn out. I had him walk past me in the street without a sign of recognition, and I had him glance at me in puzzlement and walk on. I had myself tailing him for a week or two and then, realising that there was nothing to discover, that this was all there was, returning to the hotel, packing my bags and flying home. I had myself engage him in conversation in a bar or a café, even being invited back to his flat or room. But the one constant was that I did not own up to who I was. This was partly a literary matter, for I liked the idea that my narrator might have been tailing the wrong man, and never come to realise this, though the reader would suspect it – and of course a direct confrontation would put an end to the ambiguity. But it was also a personal and psychological matter, for I now came to see, in the course of writing about it, that my notion of a reunion was completely one-sided: I wanted to find my father, but I did not want him to find me.

When I understood this I gave up the exercise. My heart wasn't really in it, anyway. The idea had seemed a good one, but deep down I experienced a kind of disgust at the thought of turning my life (and his) into a piece of fiction. I prefer to write my fiction neat, as it were, without any admixture of watery reality. So the half-hearted drafts were torn up and put in the dustbin.

And then one day he resurfaced.

His cousin phoned me with the news that he was alive and well and living in Calabria with a young woman, the centre of an admiring circle of devoted disciples. For my father, it seemed, had become a faith-healer.

He started to send the cousin his books, both printed and in manuscript, with instructions to pass these on to me. A short while later the phone rang and a female voice at the other end explained that she was a friend of my father's, that he had been following my progress with great interest and would like to renew contact. He had been very ill, she said, almost at death's door, but had pulled through. He was a remarkable man, she said, and explained how he had cured her entirely through his miraculous faith-healing powers.

His books arrived, some sent on by his cousin, others direct from Italy. I sent him one of my books in return and he wrote to say that his English was not really good enough to read what I had written but that he was struck by the photograph on the dust-jacket. He would like news of me. Why did I not come and visit?

In another letter he explained how crushed he had always been by his own father and how much better it had been for me not to have to suffer the same fate. To his cousin he wrote that he had hidden himself away for all these years out of a sense of shame at his failure to live up to his own high expectations for himself, and only re-emerged now he felt he had something to show for his life, could in fact be seen to have made a success of it. He also explained that the reason for his present ill-health was that he had been tortured by the Gestapo in an effort to get him to reveal our whereabouts. Why should the Gestapo be so interested in a mother and child? asks my cousin on the phone. And why should they catch him and then let him go? He is also saying, she reports, that he has been nominated for the Nobel Prize and that there is even talk of his eventual canonisation. Is he mad, we wonder?

The books come in two forms: novels about 'historical' personages, such as Mary Magdalene and Mesmer, written in the style of fifties movies, with Mozart making an appearance in the Mesmer book and Jesus figuring prominently in the other; and rambling essays on the True Way, combining traditional Gnosticism with bits of pseudo-science. There is also a little pamphlet, whose title consists simply of my father's name, made up of a series of essays on the man and his work by what are evidently his disciples. The first essay is called 'Who is this man?', and it is followed by 'The Master', 'The Esoteric Way' (the title of one of the books he has sent me), 'The Unpublished MSS', 'The Doctrine', 'The Therapy' and 'Concerning the Spirit'.

'Who is this man?' asks the author of the first essay. 'I do not know,' she replies, but 'I think I can testify that [he] incarnates that type of human being who is to be found, everywhere and always, whenever one has the humility to stretch out his hand to another.' 'He is the Archetype,' she continues, 'the Celestial Adam.' 'Saint?' she asks,

> Prophet? No. Jean is not a saint and he is not a prophet, he is a man like you and me, a man who teaches and reveals, by his sole presence, what each of us can realise in himself, his own proper divine descent, that each of us can become the Son of God . . . Become that which is between the Absolute and the Relative. All and Nothing.

This is daunting stuff to read about anyone, more than doubly so when it is about one's own father. A glance at the rest of the pamphlet revealed that the chapter entitled 'The Doctrine' was in fact an interview with 'the Master'. His answers to his interlocutor occasionally erupted into large print and my eye focused on some of these passages. The first principle of his doctrine, I learned, was 'TO DISCERN ONE'S OWN ESSENTIAL NEEDS'. Another was to 'ELIMINATE FROM THE SELF THAT WHICH IS NOT THE SELF'. A third was 'TO PASS FROM THE SUBJECTIVE STATE TO THE OBJECTIVE STATE'.

I kept promising myself to read through everything carefully and then write him a long and detailed letter, setting forth my reactions. But something in me kept preventing me from reading more than a few pages at a time, and meanwhile more and more manuscripts kept arriving. I therefore had to content myself with merely thanking him for the material and saying, coward that I was, that I was very much looking forward to reading it all with the care it deserved but that just at the moment, what with the novel I was working on and my teaching, I simply did not have the time.

Several months passed. I would pick up the books, determined to have a real go, then lose track after a few pages and put them down. Then one day – it was a Saturday afternoon in August and the house and streets were deserted, for everyone was down at the beach – the phone rang. I picked it up and a voice at the other end of the line said, in French: Is that Gabriel? When I said it was, the voice said: It's your father.

The phone makes me uneasy at the best of times. I feel I need to look at the person I am talking to or the experience seems unreal. When the person at the other end claims, probably rightly, to be my father, the whole thing takes on a further dimension of unreality.

However, a conversation of a sort ensues. He reproaches me for saying *vous* to him: How can you say *vous* to your own father? he asks. But *tu* is impossible for me, so I stick to the plural. He tells me of his house, in one of the most beautiful regions of Italy, close to one of the last great unspoilt forests of Europe, and urges me to come and visit: You needn't stay long. Come with a friend if you like. I thank him. He congratulates me on having had a play put on at the National Theatre. I explain that it was only a platform play and was nothing of any great consequence. He tells me that he has a great many plays in manuscript, which he would be interested to see put on. Could I use my influence at the National? I explain that I have no influence at the National, and that they unfortunately only read plays submitted in English. Why not translate some of mine? he asks. I explain that I am in the middle of a novel. Of course both our names would appear on the cover together, he says, that goes without saying. I tell him I don't know if I would ever really have the time. What I need, he says, is an agent in England. I have so much important material, he says, which a number of esoteric presses are bringing out in Italy, to great acclaim, but I need to reach people in the English-speaking world. I tell him I know nothing about agents who specialise in the esoteric, but that he should get hold of the *Writers' and Artists' Yearbook*, which lists the names of all reputable agents. If he wants I can send him a copy. No, he says, what he needs is a personal recommendation, perhaps I can look into the matter. I say I will, he repeats his invitation and rings off.

After that I felt I owed it to myself and him to read through the work carefully and write to him as honestly and yet in as friendly a way as I knew how. It seemed to me that politeness and fear were putting up barriers of false expectations which had to be pulled down quickly if our relationship was ever to develop.

This time I kept going, even though reading through the mass of material was even harder than I had anticipated. All the clichés I so dreaded were there, both in the fiction and in the essays. Of course there was no clear-cut distinction between the two. Mesmer was presented as a type of the faith-healer and Mary Magdalene's body was said to be 'inhabited by God'. In both there was the familiar mixture of Gnosticism and Kabala, though with here and there an admixture of Sufism. In both there were the usual injunctions to the reader to find the light of God within himself and to redeem his life by following 'the way'; both exuded the usual ponderous solemnity, unrelieved by wit or irony.

I wrote him a long letter, putting forward, as tentatively as I could, my objections to the doctrine and its formulation. I insisted that of course this was only my own point of view, coloured, as it always must be, by my own history and temperament. I said that I felt it was important for any future relationship between us that he should try to understand this.

Of course it was no good. He replied with an icy letter, hardly mentioning mine, but pointing out in return that my writing, in so far as he could judge it, was still rather feeble and derivative, derivative, it would seem, of Sartre, existentialism, Rilke and Jouhandeau.

I had realised that it would be easy to dismiss my criticism as being motivated by a mixture of envy and resentment, but reality always exceeds our imaginings. I tried to put myself in his place and wondered if I would react in the same way to my son's criticism of my own work, and had to admit that I might well.

A year or two later, when a novel of mine was published in an Italian translation, I asked the publishers to send him a copy. He responded with a curt note of thanks and the remark that 'it must stop'. 'It', it seemed, was the form of words I regularly use for the potted biography publishers like to have on the jackets of their books. There I say, truthfully enough, that I was born in Nice in 1940 of Russo-Italian, Romano-Levantine parents. As a naturalised Frenchman of many years, drawing a pension from the French government, he wrote, he objected strongly to my referring to him as Romanian. This, his letter suggested, could even cost him his pension. He also added that his own books had been translated into nine languages and repeated that his name had been put forward as a candidate for the Nobel Prize.

* * *

What possible contact can there be between two people of such different views, separated by twenty-six years in time and by the much wider gulf of education and cultural expectation? Why should a genetic link make it any more likely that they will see eye to eye? The fact that he is my father must mean something; yet he is, after all, a complete stranger. Worse, really, for with a complete stranger one can get on even where there are fundamental disagreements, but my father and I are complete strangers who nevertheless appear each to be making tacit claims on the other which the other rejects. What kind of a relationship can ever be established on that basis?

Bonds are not forged by genetic links but by shared experience. However liberated the woman, she will still carry the child in her body for nine months and then feed and care for it for a number more. If mother, father and child live together then bonds will be forged between them whether they like it or not. But if, as is the case with most animals, there is no link except for the genetic one between sire and offspring, we would find any show of tenderness between them very surprising. Why then should it be any different with the human animal?

For a long time in human history it was vital for the survival of the group that families be formed and maintained. In many cultures this need was given religious sanction and even religious justification. The historian, Peter Brown, has recently written with his customary eloquence of the shock-waves felt by the whole of ancient society at the emphasis placed by the new religion of Christianity on celibacy and virginity. And indeed for almost two thousand years after that the Church made sure that marriage was not downgraded by this strain in the tradition. Only in our century has the whole concept of marriage come into question as it grows clear that it is no longer necessary either economically or sociologically.

And yet 'unnatural' is far from being a dirty word in my vocabulary, and I believe we often learn how to act by playing a role. I have too much respect for the Judaeo-Christian tradition and too deep-rooted a belief if not in the sanctity of the family at least in its benefits and in its probable superiority to any other system devised by human beings, not to feel that its disappearance will entail a terrible loss. I do not believe that my grandfather's feelings at being cut off from his wife and daughters were purely sentimental. Of course it could be objected that I do not know how he felt, that it is I who am being sentimental in attributing sorrow and pain to him. No one, of course, will ever know, but no one is going to persuade me either that his sufferings were not real. Indeed, there is probably a direct link between love and suffering. My separation from my father has not entailed suffering for either of us. That is a blessing; but it is also, of course, a loss.

IN FATHERLAND

LAURIE FLYNN

He held on to his capacity for kindness until the last. Aged eighty-two and tucked up in bed in the little front room of the flat near the Botanic Gardens, he had suddenly become so agitated, so insistent that I take some money from him and obtain a volume of poems by Robert Garioch. I was pretty sure at the time that it was his way of saying 'Goodbye' and though neither of us spoke of the likelihoods, possibilities and probabilities of his impending death, we sensed, both of us, that we would probably never meet again. He touched my hand in the way he had done since I was a child and I smoothed his hair and stroked his neck. He managed a smile but it was wan, rehearsed and brave rather than joyful as his smiles had often been in the past.

I kissed him and went back to London – then, a few days later, set off for Spain. Late on Saturday night just twenty-four hours shy of the end of the seven-day package holiday, the call came from Edinburgh to say that he was gone. As I'd thought at the time, the book was his way of saying goodbye and perhaps of speaking to me from beyond the grave. He had been a bookbinder and books were important to him.

I said goodbye to my own family and caught the airport bus in front of the hotel. Leaving the little town, the bus soon began to thread its way through the Mallorean midlands where modernity is still somewhat incomplete in the exercise of its grip. It was a Sunday morning and the old, peasant people in their fine, dark clothes were on their way to mass. Outside one of the churches beyond the huddle of pensioners there was a name-plate for San Vicente, my atheist, anti-clerical father's first and very Christian name. I cried good, salt tears and sang a favourite song of his, 'She moves through the fair', simultaneously at the top of my voice and under my breath. I felt the better for the venting of my sorrow and in no time at all found myself at the airport. Explaining the circumstances repeatedly to airport traffic controllers, ticket agents, stewards and others in the departure terminal, I was soon on a flight to Glasgow without fuss or surcharge. There I rented a car and made the short, speeding journey from the city where he was born and lived to the city where he lived and died.

At my mother's house, my parents' friends Sheila and Walter Miller and my cousin Kathleen – 'John's daughter' as my dad used to say fondly, always recalling his dead brother after naming his niece – were looking after the sole remaining resident. She came to the door, crumpled, tiny into my arms. My mother. The outward signs of her sorrow were die-cast in her face. Yet no sooner had I scanned them than they were gone, repressed, banished, conjured away by a supreme act of will. She'd been well brought up, this woman, schooled by her own mother with the special sorrow of a widow left to raise two young children, one of whom was there with me now at the door.

From her earliest days, though not by choice, she had practised putting a good face on adversity, and at the age of eighty-three she was soon doing what her own wisdom and experience as well as her family line had taught her. The nurses, she began when I was inside the door, had done a lovely job – staying with her all night, making sure she was never alone. '"Just leave it all to me",' the nursing sister had said, '"and I'll have him looking beautiful in no time at all."' She had been as good as her word, my mother reported, dressing him in his best suit, with a tie of pattern and silk that had given him particular pleasure and his beloved, tan-coloured shoes, worn but beautiful. 'You know,' added my mother, 'the nurse talked to him all the time she worked on the setting out.'

I paused, distracted by the layers of meaning in the words 'setting out'. By instinct she paused with me and then she continued. 'Your father's gone,' she said calmly. For the body had been removed by the time I got there, which made the story about the nurse all the more affecting. It took away any lingering twinges of anxiety I had about seeing my dead father. I got into his old car and drove off to the Cooperative Funeral Service in Fountainbridge to say goodbye in person. In the chapel of rest I gazed at him set out in his coffin, and a line came to mind from a Sonny Terry and Brownie McGee song he had come to like nearabouts as much as I: 'You had love like the ocean rolling, that comes in with the tide'. And so he did, had it inside him and gave it out, to anyone who needed it.

Before leaving the premises, I agreed with the undertaker that he could fasten down the lid.

Back home at my mother's we talked now about Vincent's last days and hours, how difficult they'd been, how painful and extended, yet in the end dignified and at home. We wrote the little death notice for the *Scotsman*, thanking the nurses and the doctors who had come without question because of changes which my father had longed for and lived to see. Then we set to work, obtaining the death certificate and arranging the funeral. We did this with one consideration sharp in our minds. Virtually every other funeral we'd been to in recent years was as depressing as a visit to a factory farm or the prospect of a fourth, consecutive election victory for a governing party. We decided in our own amateurish way to try to restructure this occasion and join some celebration of life to this marking of death.

One friend, Michael Foreman, agreed to open the proceedings at the graveside. Fine and good looking in a Donegal tweed suit that would have reminded my father of his roots in Ireland, his voice was crisp and strong against the cold morning air. He introduced himself and called us together in congregation. Next he summoned another friend, George MacDougall, who delivered words of remembering and farewell in a voice as clear and strong as it was loving and kind. Given the situation in Scotland at the time, there were in his words tiny, tasteful echoes of political discourse. Then as the coffin was lowered into the cut in the ground, Susan Robertson, a singer of songs if ever there was one, moved to the front, brought one leg forward to brace herself against the slope, lowered her head to take in breath, closed her eyes, and began her beautiful song of parting.

> *'Swing low, sweet chariot, coming for to carry me home.*
> *Swing low, sweet chariot, coming for to carry me home.*
> *I looked over Jordan and what did I see, coming for to*
> *carry me home.*

> *A band of angels coming after me, coming for to carry me*
> *home.'*

We joined in all the choruses and muffled our tears as best we could for the verses in between, and as Susan finished it began to feel wet as well as cold for June. Thanking the diggers, we were soon across the road in the little hotel having a drink and some food to warm our souls. After about an hour and a half, the stories, pious and impious, were running out and people were ready for trains to Glasgow or homes or overnight accommodation nearer at hand. We paid the bar staff and the hotel keeper and I thought it was over.

But I reckoned without the newspapers. First the *Scotsman* wanted an obituary, so George MacDougall obliged them with one. Then the *Guardian* asked, and George was kind enough to write that too. Then the telephone went. Try as I might, it seemed I could not avoid putting pen to paper for the *Independent*:

> Extremities of poverty and social deprivation have unfortunately been part of many a twentieth-century Glasgow childhood and they decisively shaped the life of Vincent Flynn, the Glasgow socialist and trade unionist. But these social factors can lead to consciousness and kindness rather than hatred, to humanism as well as political fire. So they did with Vincent Flynn . . .

* * *

My friend Ben Ulenga, born in the Ovambo lands which straddle the border between Namibia and Angola, loved his father too. During the eight years he served of a fourteen-year sentence on Robben Island for opposing apartheid, Ben had time to think deeply about the periodic absences and irregular returns of his father who, in order to feed his family, had to leave them and journey a thousand miles to the desert wastelands in the south where diamonds were mined.

That children suffer from the rupture of routine, from the assertion and reassertion of power and authority, that the days and moments of absence were painful and those of return not always easy is something Ben captured in one of his beautiful poems, which he wrote on the island and entitled simply and directly 'Fathers'.

> *We do not want our fathers here*
> *they are strangers to us*

they only bring smells
of tobacco rolls
and sweat
from where they spend their year
far away from home

always they talk
diamonds
trains
money, mines
gold and sand dunes
these are things we've never seen . . .

As a youngster I felt resentment against fathers and fatherhood, just like Ben Ulenga. When I quarrelled with my dad, I resented him as much as I loved him. He seemed such a powerful man – big like Perry Mason, with shoulders that came from generations of work in the fields. His hands were enormous, his feet so large he could only be shod from January sales in unusual shops. Until I realised that most Scots of his generation were small and I saw the Harlem Globetrotters at the Haymarket ice rink I sometimes thought he was the biggest man in the world. Sometimes this was a source of comfort, sometimes not.

And he had another family – his union. From an early age I wanted to know about his organising, so one Saturday afternoon he took me with him to a paper mill. I can still remember the hideous noise, the all-encompassing smell. The mill had grown up on a river tributing the Forth not far away from Edinburgh, a capital city where order and government were unthinkable without reams upon reams of paper, white paper, singular and plural and watermarked and shining in its purity. On my first journey into the interior with him I discovered that paper was cooked in a vile soup of wood pulp, water and chemicals. As it boiled over into the atmosphere it produced a truly atrocious smell which caught the throat in a second, then swiftly moved to choke the lungs and cut the stomach from inside: 'Jesus, dad. I wish you hadn't taken me with you . . . I'd rather have been at home.' 'Look, son. I'm sorry,' he replied. 'But you wanted to come. And I'm glad you've seen those dark, satanic mills.'

Later he told me a story about a compensation case in which he had been involved. A boiler in one of the mills had overheated and exploded, killing a teenage girl who worked there. Her mother had sued, with the backing of the union. The girl had been disabled since birth, he said, without voice or hearing, a 'deaf mute' in the cruel discourse that dominated before the 'extravagances' of the sixties. This made the outcome of the story all the more unspeakable to an eleven-year-old boy. 'No mother should profit from the death of a daughter,' the judge had ruled.

After we moved to London, I spent more time away from my father and he from me. My plans for Saturdays stretched to include evenings on my own, spread outwards into Fridays, Sundays and then beyond even those once impregnable boundaries. With each expansion of horizon I seemed to have a greater need for small amounts of money, which I obtained from a succession of jobs beginning with a paper round and ending with a half-day's work in a bookie's in Brixton each and every Saturday. This was a job of which he disapproved, famously, on moral and political grounds. (Until I told him the rate of pay. Then he softened – a little.)

One way and another those late teenage years included some major conflicts, some memorable rows. I would stop out. I would forget to say when or even if I would be home. For a brief while there seemed an almost limitless variety of causes for disputes – my first tentative encounters with poverty as a problem and petty dishonesty as a transitory solution; my first bouts of drink; my first all-night parties; my first CND march. In the mornings of my growing freedom I was not always in prime condition; and it took me a little time to understand that there might be some genuinely legitimate basis for concern about my whereabouts.

As this realisation dawned I found that my parents could be more open to messages from the other side. I tried to explain that I didn't always want people to know where I was going. I was experimenting, freewheeling, trying the world. Sometimes when I set out, goddammit, I didn't even know where I was going. 'I mean, Vincent. Have you heard of the youth revolt or what?' 'Are birds free from the chains of the skyway?' 'Please, dad? Lend me a pound!'

In the end we seemed to reach towards a new balance. Their seed had become its own flower, for better or for worse. I moved away, I lived on my own, in my own space . . . in various rooms which reminded my dad of 'single ends', 'rooms and kitchens' and other marketing concepts devised by the Glasgow slumlords of his youth.

After he retired and returned to Edinburgh he began telling me how to get from George Street to Princes Street in a town where I had lived for years, where I'd had a paper round (with all its attendant depth of knowledge) and which I'd navigated daily to go to school. As he grew older I even began to use my driving licence and somewhat individual-istic driving skills to take him for little outings. Thanks to the extra-ordinary poverty of his youth he had little lung function, and access to a motor car prolonged his life by decades, bringing him pleasure even after he had ceased to have the confidence to drive.

After he broke his hip and walking became difficult, such outings became even more important. His favourite was to travel east through Leith out along the coast road to visit Luca's ice-cream shop in Musselburgh on a Sunday afternoon. Arriving there we could be sure we'd have difficulty parking and be obliged to join an exceptionally long queue. It was always worth the sweat, for the beauty of the ice-cream as well as the sweetness of the smile it brought to his lips.

On the way home he'd ask me which way I was going to go and then immediately give me directions. For some reason buried deep in the pain of the middle passage, this always used to annoy me. And I confess that after he was gone, I remarked quietly to myself that I would never get such directions again. I was wrong. My mother took over the role.

* * *

Some months after Vincent died I found my own way to Waterstone's bookshop in George Street. There amid the stacks was a new issue of *Granta*, that mother and father of British literary magazines whose design and typography I admired and whose contents I periodically savoured and enjoyed. This encounter was to be something of an exception. The title page, reversed out against a background some would call aubergine, others maroon, was simple and direct and called out across the room: 'They fuck you up'. The setting was delicate, cunning and opportunistic in lower case and doubtless the result of considerable tactical debate.

The back cover carried further and better particulars and capitalised on the letters: 'THEY FUCK YOU UP – The Family'. Then the marketing message filled out as follows:

'They fuck you up your mum and dad' Philip Larkin wrote, but Philip Larkin got it wrong.

There are also your brothers and your sisters. And your uncles, your grandfather, your endless cousins, your second cousins, your mother-in-law, your father-in-law and your children. There are always your children.

Except for one optimistic piece (about yachting), the articles inside were a cheap celebration of the pathological, and were poor at probing even that.

Looking back over my own journeyings through fatherlands and motherlands, and even making huge depreciation allowances for all the problems and imperfections, the sheer wear and tear and friction of human interaction, I have memories of parents who managed to extend their kindnesses and sense of possibility to many other children in the neighbourhood. We were all 'Jock Thamson's bairns', each of us a message to the future and a special gift to the world. Families were shelters from storms as well as centres of storms. They propped you up rather than fucked you up.

*　*　*

Now, especially now that I must make some limited sense of death, I keep seeing the pathways of kindness rather than the hard shoulder of cruelty. (I heard the news again today, oh boy, and read about it in the printed tide of morning.) Even many of the conflicts and rows that I experienced make some sort of sense as I steel myself to re-enact them or some of them with those children I live among and directly influence for better and for worse.

Their names are *Rosanne* (called for the sound of the name, for a lovely woman friend I haven't seen in years and in memory of my father's mother, a woman neither he nor I ever knew); and Ewan (named for a character in a remarkable series of novels, *Sunset Song*, *Cloud Howe*, *Grey Granite*). One of them is nearly as tall as my father was, though only thirteen years old and already a devourer of books. The other is a giant of ten years, tough at times and douce just like his grandfather and with similar independence of mind.

What will their inheritance be? From fatherland? From motherland? With luck a capacity for health and freedom, a character structure that enables them to actualise themselves, to play and be joyful and to partake of an unforced, everyday generosity of giving.

*　*　*

Some weeks ago a young man with a broad Scots accent and the enchanting name Gino di Placido finished lettering a piece of grey granite and set it into the walls of the Dean cemetery in Edinburgh. Placed between weathered tablets for a stockbroker and a minister, it reads, softly, in characters let into the stone and picked out in black paint:

> Here lies Vincent Flynn, 1909–1991.
> Trade unionist and socialist.
> A good man who loved human rights.

Besides neurotic, wholly unjustified anxieties that Gino di Placido might make a mistake in a form of printing where there is little opportunity for either proof-reading or correction, I worried if this was an appropriate tribute to the peasant skills my dad brought to life. But somehow I think it signals his hopefulness, his faith in reason and his endless, incorrigible repetition in one form or another of the idea that self-government was the province of individuals as well as countries, of garbage collectors as well as the designers of evening gowns. All his grown life he dreamed of cities where there was kindness and equality as well as justice and freedom. The dreams tended to take overtly political form. But the 'politics' drew its vigour and lasting strength from springs way below the topsoil of any purely or even predominantly 'political' culture.

The strength and vigour came, it seems to me now, from a well of passion and compassion which I can only describe, somewhat pretentious though the phrase may be, as an ontology of kindness. Dostoevsky would have understood. 'I have seen the truth,' he said. 'It is not as though I had invented it with my mind. I have seen it, *seen it* and the living image of it has filled my soul for ever . . . In one day, one hour, everything could be arranged at once! The chief thing is to love.'

HIS BALLS

Noah Richler

I must have been about five or six when I first took a pee with my
father, or first remember it, sharing the same toilet bowl. I guess
I came up to about his thigh, my scrotum barely descended, and
my little penis like a pert nipple which I had to point well upwards to
get the pee over the rim of the bowl; his, meanwhile, a mammoth
sausage weighing heavy in his hand, the urine falling noisily. I remember the shadow of his enormous dick to the left of my eye. I thought:
I'll never be so big.

I love my Pa. I can't think of anything better than to be like him. He
is a writer, an artist, one of the best. Not somebody who writes novels
to prove he can do it, or because he thinks that he should, but one who
can do nothing else. If I want to write, it's probably because I love him,
not the work. I don't know. I've stopped asking. Better just to get on
with it. 'Do you want to be a writer, or to write?' he said to me, when
at thirteen I first announced a literary intention. And I remember a
garden party my parents threw when we still lived in London, some
years earlier. I was about eight, and I had just been introduced to the
Irish novelist, Edna O'Brien. I ran into the kitchen excitedly:

'Mommy, Mommy,' I said. 'I've just met a writer!'

'But darling,' my mother said, 'your father's a writer.'

'Yeah,' I whined, 'but not a *real* one.'

This idea was eroded somewhat when a TV film crew visited the
house – and especially when they filmed my father dropping my brother

and me off at school (in front of all my friends) – and my mind was pretty well changed when he took me with him to Paris, on my own. And let me tell you, it's a big thing in a family of five kids, to travel alone with your Pa. Me, all of ten years old. There we hung around the Left Bank together, supped with Mavis Gallant, and he gave me a watch that had belonged to Terry Southern, one of a group of writers my father had known when he'd lived in Paris as a young man. My father, twenty-odd, making it. I can remember, early on, the two of us looking up at the Tour d'Eiffel (he says l'Arc de Triomphe).

'Do you want to go up?' my father asked. No, I answered, I was scared of heights. 'Me too,' he said, and we went off happily together for a walk that lasted three full days, to cafés, to markets, and to the book stalls along the banks of the Seine.

My Pa didn't really talk to me, except to explain why we were at a certain restaurant, or occasionally to refer to an old pal – Terry usually, or Mason, or Ted, my Ma; but I soaked it up: Pa, looking for a tomato or a piece of good fruit; our tiny table for two at Chez Allard, smoky and noisy and busy and gay, the rich dark colour of that first *coq au vin* and the matching oak-panelled walls; or the seeming generosity of whirling French waiters, who brought baskets filled with croissants to our pavement tables. I would watch as my father argued with them vociferously, adamant that I'd not eaten four or five (it was a while before I figured out the basket was not all paid for). And there was the tiny hotel where we stayed, with the crooked flights of stairs or a slow lift hardly big enough for the two of us, the Relais Bisson, which I knew from the picture book *Eloise in Paris*. That was where he tried to explain the business of sex to me, Dad at the window of our petite and elegant pink room, looking down to the flowery courtyard:

'You know how . . .'

'Yes,' I lied, abruptly cutting him off.

'Right. Good.'

Then off to the backstreets for another morning walk, more croissants, and more of the prettily wrapped sugar cubes from the various cafés to add to my collection. That trip, more than anything, made me want to write: wandering dreamily about a beautiful city with nowhere in particular in mind, and the savoury pleasure of observing my father observing.

In England, my father embarrassed me by refusing to take me to perform in a school choir recital through a dense English fog. 'Snow I can handle,' he said. 'You don't get fog like this in Canada', and when I was twelve we moved to that other place.

In Canada, where suddenly my name was well known, there was no question my father was a writer, a real one, and it was something of a nuisance. He should have told me a bit more about being Jewish; maybe I wouldn't have attended my first bar mitzvah in a windbreaker and Adidas, or maybe he was just having a bit of a laugh. At any rate, I got into a scuffle, but was pleased that it was on his behalf. It was a strange business, the bar mitzvah. Jeremy, the boy who brought his own packed lunch every day to King's House, the school I'd attended in Richmond, had been as odd to me as he was to the rest of my classmates, though in Canada I discovered we had Jewishness in common. I discussed this with my Ma, a Roman Catholic, while my father worked upstairs. My sister, educated at a convent, entered the kitchen to collect her toast. 'You think you're Jewish?' she said bemused. 'That's interesting', and went out again. Later, the film of my father's novel *The Apprenticeship of Duddy Kravitz* was made. I hung around the set, berated one time when I talked too freely to the press. The movie was shot around St Urbain's, the old Montreal Jewish ghetto, and Pa took me to Wilensky's for a Special and cherry cola from the soda bar. He took me to a synagogue for Yom Kippur, and to my grandmother's, where I learned a little more about being Jewish (but not very much). He spoke at the high school I attended – a good turn because otherwise I'd have been in real trouble for the classes I'd missed – and he defended me in juvenile court on a vandalism charge. I remember being astonished at his eloquence – how I wish I could recollect it for you here – and the mess he made of the patronising judge, feeling triumphant and proud as we left hand in hand through the corridors of bitching couples waiting for divorces. That was the first time he really impressed me.

* * *

My psychoanalytical history is an easy one to figure; I loved my Mom, but wanted to do good for Pa (I often wondered if my father, delivering groceries around the ghetto as a kid, would have liked me at a similar age). Books made me fall asleep, especially in the house, except for Graham Greene's, and my father's. I read *Cocksure*, and *St Urbain's Horseman*, and *Duddy Kravitz* under the table at high school – his first novel, *The Acrobats*, he wouldn't let me see. The only work of his he ever gave me to read was a story about his Pa called 'My Father's Life'. I tried to write myself, but only succeeded in letters. One of these was to Valerie, an early siren, whose father claimed to have been a schoolmate of Dad's.

'Sure, I remember him,' said Pa when I checked up. 'If the exams were any tougher he'd still be there.' Valerie's brother was a classmate of mine, and he would take copies of *Duddy Kravitz* (a set text at the school), and burn them in front of me, page by page. No matter, I thought, one less return and a few more royalties. The letter to Valerie was steamy, lusty, even pornographic, filled with sexual details I knew only at secondhand. Fiction, I suppose. I wrote it in the basement one night when the parents were out, managing to get drunk from the one-shot liquor bottles they'd amassed from their many flights, usually back to England. When I spilled wine on the letter by accident, I called it a night, left the four stained pages on the kitchen table to dry, and went off to bed.

In the morning, the pages were not there. My father called me up to the office, the place high above us where he worked, to which I had carried tea since a small child, where we went only with permission, and the reason why I had to be quiet when I played with my brothers and sisters. Humbly I took my place before the sturdy roll-top desk, where a few months before (Farley's book-burnings in mind), I had asked how he made his money. 'None of your business,' he said, probably not wanting to encourage me in a difficult profession, and that was that. Later, I rummaged around, a scoundrel naturally. I found the carbon copy of a deal with a Midwestern university for some of his papers to be bequeathed *seven years after my death*. In my sleep that night I had a phone call from afar. It was my father, long distance, on one of his many trips. 'Noah,' he said, 'I'm dying.' Then the line broke. It was what you call a nightmare, and it did recur. That was the last time I peeked among his papers, scattered then as usual in their mysterious and only apparently disorderly piles, overlapping, everywhere.

'Who is Valerie?' my father asked.

'My girlfriend,' I said.

'Are you going to send this letter to Valerie?'

'Yes,' I said.

'You know that Valerie will read this to all her friends, and that you'll be the laughing-stock of the school, don't you?'

'Yes,' I said.

'And you're still going to send it?'

'Yes,' I said.

'Well then,' my father replied, picking up the letter from the desk.

'You use the word *fuck* four times. If you used it only once it would have far more effect.'

That was the first advice on writing my father ever gave me (and soon after that I broke into Valerie's house to retrieve the letter). Another time he told me not to blow the punch line, once to say what you mean, another time to listen to how people speak, and some time recently he asked me, after an enthusiastic book review I had written for an English daily, if I really felt so strongly about the book. 'He uses so many adjectives,' he said. 'It takes two pages for him to tell you it rained.' Pithy is my father's style, as when, having sent home from Asia a box of clothes I did not need on my long voyage, I received a telegram in Kuala Lumpur which read: DO YOUR OWN LAUNDRY. To my brother, who showed him the first draft of his novel (which I would never do), he said, 'I've never read a novel which couldn't be cut by a hundred pages', though later, when I told him I'd written a story which was seventy pages long and I didn't know where to try and place it, he said, 'what you do is give one character a stutter, and make another deaf, and you've got a novella. You'll learn these tricks in time.'

I did show him a piece of writing once, when I was particularly distraught at high school, in which I described the frenzied beating of a woman. He summarily dropped it from the couch where he lay each afternoon eating herring and tomatoes – and where he lay one time when I'd come in dripping wet and fulminating at the drivers who'd failed to pick me up hitch-hiking in a heavy rainfall: 'the world doesn't owe you a living,' he'd said typically. I watched it fall to the floor, where I would have to retrieve it from the day's discarded papers and magazines, and he said something curt and dismissive. Whatever the words, they were uttered so quickly that I hardly heard them, though I understood the tone. I just remember being angry that he had missed a message that wasn't even between the lines, my motherfucker. As a teenager, sex was difficult for me, and I experienced some impotence for a time. When I told my Pa directly, he was sympathetic. 'It's scary,' he said, 'and a man can't go comparison shopping. You have no reason to feel secure.' Then he told me some anecdote to make me feel better, about a government minister at his first Cabinet meeting who had confided to Pearson, the Prime Minister, about just how nervous he was. And so am I, replied Pearson the old hand, apparently. (I don't remember the book he was reading at the time.)

Man, the business of parenting is something. Even in my late twenties, older than my father was when he had me, watching my little brother grow up I knew that I would have made all the wrong decisions. Surely I would never have had the wisdom, or the patience – and there were five of us!

We weren't easy.

As a kid I travelled, I skipped school, I took drugs. 'You leave the taps on,' my father would say. 'Every day you make lunch and you leave it on the counter. You leave doors open. What's wrong?' He probably knew what was wrong but my mother must have held him back. Instead he fixed up a job for me in the Yukon as a prospector's assistant, and sent me off for a summer above the tree line with Dostoevsky, Koestler and Stendahl, but also Ring Lardner and *The Art of Kissing*. I made a lot of money, and the Yukon changed my life, but it was going to be a while before I was finished with the druggy road, although it wasn't until I came back from Asia to Montreal that I became more seriously involved with drugs. I appeared one day at the country house with an earring and a shaved head. I had been away for a year. My father turned, visibly moved at his son's return, but he was also taken aback. 'The earring,' he asked. 'It doesn't *mean* anything, does it?' 'No,' I said. 'I'm not gay.'

In Montreal, I became dependent. There were varying reasons, and I change my mind from time to time assessing them. Generally I think it's because the encapsulation of all that teenage angst into a single, tangible and physically painful needle-point made me feel good, special even in my grief. It was also kind of cerebral – I mean I was well read about it, conscious of precedent, well versed in Crowley and De Quincey, Lewis Carroll and Samuel Taylor Coleridge. 'Sister Morphine', the memorable Stones number, also played some part, and so did the travellers returning from Asia before I'd left, but it was Dad on Terry Southern and Mason Hoffenberg really, and that watch; and damned if I wasn't going to know the daemon for myself.

That summer I worked at a delicatessen, throwing up in the toilet in the basement of Ben's between runs for more orders of coleslaw. I told the folks eventually (as if they didn't know), and the summer was like Camp David. I would travel from the city and my business there to the house in the country where they spent Canada's few hot months by the lake, to sit and talk with my parents – voluntarily. Try and work it out. My father, sipping his customary deep glass of Scotch, would keep his patience for a time, then he would yell at me; my mother would chair.

Some time later, he took me with him to New York. It was the first time I had been alone with him on a trip since he'd taken me to Paris some ten years before. The Algonquin, he told me, was overbooked, and at the doors of a sleazier hotel on Lexington Avenue, he stopped me. Not wanting me to be taken for a rent-boy by the staff, he pointed to my earring. 'No jewellery,' he said.

We went out together. To the theatre and for walks, and to bookshops, though not to markets. But I remember most vividly lying on our twin beds one evening in the hotel room, the 2/4 clicking of the neon sign outside the window, and the sirens rising from the night-time street below. My father lay wearily, tired I think because of travel, the long day, work, and me. He appeared distracted, lost in thought, and the atmosphere was peaceful. We did not speak for a long while, until my father interrupted the silence.

'I don't understand why you do it, Noah,' he said. 'If you saw what happened to Mason. I used to have to take him into the bathroom and hold his veins for him to find them with the needle. I watched him waste away. He was so talented. I don't understand why you do it.'

I watched my father, full of love. He paused and then he said, 'I've had a marvellous life. I love my wife, I have wonderful children, and I'm good at my work. Life for me is like . . . is like biting into a piece of fresh fruit. A tomato. I don't know why you do it.'

My father and his tomatoes. Firm, red tomatoes.

I got out of it pretty quickly after that, found a girl for whom the bruised veins meant nothing, and learned to fuck instead of shoot a needle. Now, occasionally, my father and I have words, at Christmas-time usually, on some important issue like work or land, or when he's put up to it by my Ma. Like the time when he visited me in London recently, his London, where I live away from the family now, and he knew that I was struggling in love. 'So,' he said, leaning on his usual deep glass of Scotch, 'how's it going with N?', which sounded ridiculous from him. Anyway, I was pleased that he asked, and my balls more or less in order, I answered, gushing, but this was his turn to cut me off, this gruff, steady, rock of a man, who wanted to share a drink though not necessarily to talk. 'It takes a little work, you know,' he said. 'I mean I didn't get your mother just like *that*.'

Sure, Pa. It takes a little work. And the family, not the work, is the project.

DRUIDS, PRIESTS, BARDS AND OTHER FATHERS

OWEN DUDLEY EDWARDS

G od exists. Therefore it was necessary to invent Him.
If we can only conceptualise a creator of the universe in the vocabulary of earthed gender, God the Mother would make more visible sense, as it evidently did to many ancient civilisations: a Mother-creator of life is a visible phenomenon, a Father-creator is invisible in his flashpoint of creativity (even when flashing). But fatherhood, biologically needless save for the moment of fertilisation, wrote itself into the lead part by mystification. God was He.

Fatherhood happens in a moment of male pleasure, to be followed at the end of nine months by female agony. The Judaeo-Christian tradition disposed of any belittlement of the status of fatherhood by demanding the mother's post-natal purification, until which point she was unclean and unfit for decent society. So having done all the work, the woman must then take all the guilt. Through much of human history, fatherhood has also been the sole pleasure in procreation: the majority of children born since the creation of the world could well be the products of rape, or at best of male importuning and female acquiescence falling below consent or desire. Most marriages in human history have been the result of man-made bargains, sometimes with the woman holding no acquaintance with her predetermined husband until her father/brother has sealed her into the bargain in terms acceptable to him. So procreation within marriage has been legalised rape, probably in a majority of cases since the dawn of time.

Fatherhood, whether achieved because of or in default of the acqui-escence of its female target, may exculpate itself theologically or otherwise from the travail of childbearing and parturition, may choose also to emancipate itself from the literally dirty work of infant care; but fatherhood has its own strong motives for taking its role seriously according to its priorities. Whether the father believes in some form of personal immortality or not, fatherhood has traditionally seen itself as a form of insurance for survival beyond the grave. Its intentions are for the child, especially the male child, to continue its forms of self-assertion. Ideally, the father will perpetuate himself down the gener-ations whether by means of land ownership, or even claim to long-lost land or status asserted in exile, in poverty or in hereditary tenancy; in guardianship of craft secrets; in vendetta or obligation; in religious, patriotic and/or ideological legacy; or in vaguer but no less passionately supported tradition. Fatherhood usually feels itself more secure by choice of a sympathetic female vessel to bear his purchase on immortal-ity: the necessary sympathy may not be required in the initial act of procreation, and the folklore of male chauvinism of the taming-of-the-shrew variety indicates a frequent preference for the acquisition of such sympathy by conquest, violent or psychological, but the basic assump-tion requires agreement by the mother in the transmission of the particular paternal values. Hence the emphasis on a partner from the tribe, neighbourhood, religion, country, class, and so on. There are counter-pressures: personal fortunes are open to betterment by mar-riage to a female of superior status, or by advantageous economic or other alliances outside the aspirant father's associates of common interest, kinship, craftsmanship, class, religion, geographical location or point of supposed origin. If the counter-pressures prevail, the taming process may be more protracted, but in theory all is to be resolved by the inaugurating act of fatherhood.

The arrival of the male child at the use of Reason, or his enforced participation in rites of passage, or his formal coming of age, or whatnot, asserts his formal state of readiness for the reception of his father's priorities in perpetuating him. But these terms are modern reworkings of the ancient occasions for a boy's breaking in to appren-ticeship for his father, and worlds dominated by physical prowess demanded recruitment at a much earlier age than those in which coming of age was marked by the Squire inviting the tenantry to pledge their young master or the family solicitor requiring his signature to major documents. The other remote antecedent of coming of age presumed physical maturity by the boy-child, but sometimes with the implicit agenda of supplanting his father, if necessary by his death. Hence the traditions of fatherhood involve the father's hopes of immortality by the creation of sons becoming alternated with the furtherance of his existence by the destruction of sons. Much of human history has turned on the problems of the period lying between those points before which the son poses no obvious threat to the life of the father, and after which the father poses none to that of the son. Each wishes to move the points to their own advantage, one earlier, one later. Social wisdom recognises the danger of such wishes: Abraham may sacrifice Isaac with the boy's unwitting compliance, but he should not; Absalom, if he strikes for power too early, must be destroyed. We all grow more sophisticated, and a generation of power-hungry Absaloms can be profitably thinned by their fathers' wars: David had shown the way, if not in his struggle against Absalom – the method had disposed of Bathsheba's inconvenient husband. Leslie Charteris's Simon Templar summed it up neatly enough in his 'The Noble Sportsman': 'it's part of the psychology of war, whether you like it or not, that war is the time when the old men come back into their own, and the young men who are pressing on their heels are miraculously removed' (*The Saint Intervenes*, 1934). Fatherhood seeks immortality, or at least posthumous perpetuation, as Augustine sought chastity: devoutly, but not yet.

Social control, notably as expressed by druids, priests and bards, has traditionally maintained a fine balance between the spiritual and physical perpetuations of the father. In theory, it preached piety with powerful sanctions against patricide: in practice, it looked indulgently at exhibitions of independence, teenage rebellion, ritualistic forgatherings with objects of paternal dislike on the assumption that once the father's physical survival or at least authority demanded more of society than it gave, the son might supplant the father provided he then forsook his own past and assumed his father's. Oedipus, although an unwitting and unwilling patricide (no Oedipus complex there), must be punished and ousted; but Prince Hal, despite his premature self-coronation, may enter into his kingdom provided he sloughs off his rebellion by the punishment and ousting of his former accomplices. He may disown his real father and follow a surrogate father, but he must become his real father by turning his patricidal inclinations against the surrogate father.

Absalom's mistake lay not in rebellion against his father but in failing to slay Achitophel.

Shakespeare asserted the independence of his artistry by his progress from *Henry IV* and *Henry V* to *Hamlet*. How can a Renaissance intellectual tie himself to a primeval revenge tradition when he has hardly known the father he is supposed to avenge? Ignorance of his father might have its uses – Hamlet could wallow in a cult of the dead King to feel personal prejudices against a successor whose sensible preferences for diplomacy above war should have commanded his intellectual respect – but when invited by the Ghost to get down to business he is confronted by problems of the Ghost's identity and apparently has no common memories on which to draw to settle the matter. Apart from the theological difficulty that he is a student at a Protestant university confronted by a spirit declaring itself customarily to inhabit a Catholic Purgatory and imbued with heartily pagan traditions of vengeance (which may carry a nice theological point that King Hamlet was condemned to remain in Purgatory until he learned to forgive his enemies), Hamlet is an artistic creation of an age when princes scarcely knew their fathers.

The traditions and superstitions of fatherhood hardened around an ancient core from a time when fathers did train their sons in the business of becoming themselves, as hunters, cave artists or whatever. Sophistication and specialisation delegated much of this to surrogate fathers, and kingship or chieftainship was one of the earliest activities to produce it. Celtic chieftainship put sons in fosterage, and the resultant mutations were acknowledged to the extent of entailing succession in acceptability rather than primogeniture. Societies seeking to consolidate kingship by dependence on primogeniture risked breaks in tradition by sons whose experience distanced them from the paternal impress. The great terror of fatherhood, that it is not, contrary to what it imagines, true fatherhood, blazes down on us across millennia in the savage penalties against female adultery, but progress encouraged filial search for surrogate fathers where no procreational ambiguities might have existed. The development of a culture of fatherhood itself demanded intellectual and spiritual exposition beyond most fathers' capabilities, and hence came the dependence on the bard, the cleric, the tutor, whose paternity might occasionally be more than surrogate in any case: Franz Bengtson offers the mocking example of a promiscuous tutor let loose in a Viking community in his *The Long Ships*. But that kind of thing was aberrant. The irony remains that the huge apparatus of the cult of fatherhood was largely built up by tradition-transmitters whose chief role lay outside fatherhood on their own part, and in the medieval west was formally interdicted from such activity. Clerical celibacy may have evolved, probably did evolve, less from the demands of Christ than from those of Caesar, once Caesar had conscripted the cause of Christ in his own service. The eunuch had a comparable function in other civilisations. The seminaries, boarding schools and universities continued the training in fatherhood by professional intellectuals after the Reformation. Fatherhood became too important to be left to the fathers, who assumed their own hopes of immortalisation to be strengthened by removing its instruments from their own fashioning.

Secularisation invited the apotheosis of fatherhood by the removal of God, initially transformed into a divine justification of fatherhood, but potentially a dangerous competitor. Fatherhood successively eliminated the Pope, the clergy and ultimately God from challenge and the formerly clerical intellectuals became simply salaried servants. Social structure sought to strengthen its status divisions by emphasis on the deference fatherhood demanded. Yet at the heart of the deepest self-assertion by fatherhood lay its own tacit abdication of its business of self-reproduction in spiritual if not in physical form.

But such abdication was implicit in ancient tradition. The closer we examine fatherhood, historically, the more we find its obsession with trappings, its evasion of substance. Christianity is based on a belief that the founder of the religion was the child of no earthly father, and however much feminists may dislike the absurdity with which Catholic Christianity distanced Christ's Mother into an object of prettified unreality, the heart of the faith requires her acknowledgement as sole earthly progenitor. Yet the very gospels of Matthew and Luke which describe Christ's nativity lay out long genealogies recording the descent of Joseph, husband of Mary, from Abraham (Matthew, i: 1–17) or from Adam (Luke, iii: 23–38), while making it clear in the adjoining verses that Joseph had no part in the generation of Christ. It is as though Matthew and Luke acknowledged that fatherhood had to have something with which to preen itself while conveying the principle of a Messiah completely undercutting the principle. And the contemplation of those texts may offer a suitable metaphor for the history of fatherhood: a perennial assertion of its own magnificence which is essentially irrelevant to the realities. If we require a twentieth-century evangelist, Sean O'Casey has obliged us in *Juno and the Paycock*.

To say this is not to ridicule Joseph, who was not responsible for the scriptural space given to his ancestry. It is a great pity that more fathers did not adopt his example of quiet support. But the first truth every father needs to learn is that whatever his place in the procreation of his formal offspring, it is essentially inferior to that of the mother at all important points. Even when the father took his agenda as his own duty by early apprenticeship of a son, he had no means of setting aside the real inculcation of human realities in the child by its mother from its first moments. We may not agree with psychiatry's conclusions about a child's early years, but it is surely correct in signalling their pre-eminence. If there is one factor, more than all others, which ensures that history can never be more than guesswork, it lies in our ignorance of the most important years of its subjects' lives and the manner in which impressions are made on them. All we can say is that the mother in the overwhelming majority of instances must have far more to do with making the child what it becomes than does the father.

The cult of fatherhood in its expression is therefore a roaring cataract of pernicious nonsense down the centuries, and however liberated individual fathers may be, it is inescapable. A modern father may change his infant's nappies without question, his father may have regarded any such work as emasculation but might accept a symbolically supportive role in public, *his* father may have refused under any circumstances to walk alongside the pram containing his offspring and pushed by his wife: so we have progress of a kind, though the thought of priding oneself on not descending to the level of our male ancestors is as ludicrous as priding ourselves on superiority in technology unknown to them and now within the grasp of everyone. In some ways our situation is more dangerous; priding ourselves on our modern emancipation may easily blind us to the huge survivals of the fatherhood cult and the way we implicitly or explicitly venerate it. Fathers now often share in the incredible thrill of participation in the initial care of infants, and thereby may convince themselves that in their persons fatherhood has truly found its identity and hence sometimes motherhood can once more be discounted or diminished in significance in the old ratio under a new vocabulary of liberation. The new status of feminism and the respect or fear it has engendered can enable the father simply to enlarge his prospects for self-perpetuation, and those of his male ancestors with imagination had often recognised as much: 'my daughter is as good as any man (i.e. my daughter is me)'. Freudianism may enshrine fatherhood's delusions more than its realities. Oedipus complexes and Electra complexes are probably much rarer than Freud supposed, but a Laius complex – the father's fear of being killed and supplanted by his son – is probably very widespread, if not specifically sexually oriented, and while Agamemnon, unlike Laius, had no noticeable interest in his daughter's reactions, fatherhood has long counted on Electra-fication often with as little trouble about the daughter as Agamemnon. The fact that Agamemnon had sacrificed Electra's elder sister Iphigeneia is not felt to stand in the way of Electra's devotion to him, and if anything even enhances it: so runs the fatherhood tradition. Our interest in the *Oresteia* is sufficiently sharpened by the murders of Agamemnon and Clytemnestra to obscure the element of sibling rivalry: but it is strongly within the myth in its fortification of fatherhood.

It is allied to one of the most prevalent and nauseous of all diseases of paternity, one which has prompted its counterpart from maternity, the stress on the 'favourite child'. We can behold in the 'favourite child' the embodiment of the self-perpetuation urge, a useful side-bet if primogeniture looked like failing in specific instances to work sufficiently for paternal immortality, an identification with the male first-born if that looks like serving the purpose. A mother's reasonable desire to offset the omnipresence of fatherhood and its long-term agenda creates her response in fatherhood's coinage, often successfully: and with her superior if less visible advantages she ensures her Jacob and not his Esau gets birthright and blessing whereby the father Isaac has expected to bribe posterity. But the practical horror of the situation is endless in its ramifications, especially for any third child left behind in the favouritist stakes sharpened by parental warfare. Any parent who even thinks of having a 'favourite child' is guilty of spiritual infanticide.

THE LONELINESS OF THE LONG-DISTANCE FATHER

ROGER SCRUTON

'F atherhood' names a biological relation, and also a social role. We are moral creatures, whose roles can be sundered from the needs that first gave rise to them. They then cease to be bound by animal impulses and become values, ideals and sources of authority. It may even happen that the role is most completely filled by someone who frees himself entirely from the biological imperative. The title 'father' sticks more fast to the priest who refrains from fathering than it does to the man who begets children. 'Father' is a spiritual title, and celibacy the most appropriate way of earning it.

Even as a spiritual idea, however, fatherhood involves the masculine gender. In the religions from which our civilisation derives, God is universal father and therefore male. To imagine God as female is to imagine a different God, for it is to imagine a different relation (a different *moral* relation) between God and the world. The offspring of a mother issue from her body and are part of her. A mother becomes vulnerable in her children, is subsumed by them and identifies with their joys and sufferings. The offspring of a father arise outside his body, grow at a distance from him both physically and emotionally, are subject to his observation, and fall under his tutelage.

When God the Father destroys his creation he does not destroy himself, as a mother would, but only reaffirms himself as something higher. So God rebuked the world by flooding it. This does not mean that a Divine Father loves less than a Divine Mother; but he loves more severely. His love takes the form of law: 'thou shalt', and 'thou shalt not'. His children must *earn* his love through their obedience. His voice sounding within them has the tone of a command, while the voice of a mother is ever soft with new excuses.

A mother is vulnerable *in* her children; a father is vulnerable *to* them. For he runs the risk of rebellion. To adopt his role is to become a judge, to assume the rightness of his own position, and a title to obedience. It is to close a door on all excuses, and to make justice and mercy his own. The father's position, therefore, is supremely lonely. Of course, the priest who is father to his flock can rest his case in a higher power. Father upon father stand in rank behind him, on the ladder of authority that reaches up to God. But in a godless world fathers suffer a dreadful loss of confidence. What if the only ground of my command is that I command it? Can I still cast my love as an edict, and expect my children to shape themselves through their obedience?

The question is not rhetorical: it has been part of western experience since the Enlightenment. Through belief in the Divine Father and his many earthly regents, our ancestors established a unique civilisation, in which law replaced the claims of mere emotion, and durable institutions sprang from the fertile womb of society. These institutions were often conceived in feminine terms: the mother church, the Alma Mater, the 'mother of parliaments', and so on. But they owed their longevity, their personality and their character-forming power to the law that governed them. A dialogue arose, between the active force of law, and the passive sense of membership. Neither could exist alone. Our obedience to law is purchased by the offering of home: it is because we *belong* here that the law has authority over us. And it is because the law protects us that we can build our home.

I do not say that rebellion against the father began all at once and without historical precedent. The seeds of rebellion are sown precisely in the act of procreation. But they may remain dormant for centuries, awaiting the change of climate that causes them to sprout. Suddenly the father and his law are mocked and hissed from the stage, and in his place comes a child-made substitute: an all-providing, all-excusing mother, whose female name (*la patrie*, or *la nation*, as it happened) expresses a new, permissive and inclusive bond of membership. A new hope enters the world. With the nation or the nanny state in charge, the children think, no one will be shut out, no one rebuked or disciplined. Those who defy the law cease to be criminals and are re-baptised as victims of the old oppressive order. The aim of life is no longer to grow up and assume life's burdens, but to remain attached to the nipple through which the milk of human kindness inexhaustibly flows.

The new attitude came in many guises and over many decades. Two centuries separate the rebellions of Rousseau and the Revolutionaries from those of Sartre and Foucault; a century and a half lies between Blake's God-defying Jesus and the permissive religions of the sixties. Nevertheless, a process sprang up in the Enlightenment which has continued with accelerating momentum to our day. Its single most important aim has been the unmasking and dethroning of the father, and his replacement by the mother as social archetype and true provider of our common good. Authority, law, punishment – all are exposed as mere oppression. At the same time new forms of community are proposed, from the idylls of Fourier and Robert Owen, through the 'full communism' of Marx, to the *'groupe en fusion'* of Sartre, whose ruling principle is that they have no ruling principle, and whose one source of cohesion is the fullness and freedom of untutored love.

Not everyone has gone along with the process. Here and there a father figure has proposed himself. But in the absence of the Supreme Father who ratifies his judgements, the merely human father suffers a chill of isolation. In the art and literature of the nineteenth century his power and authority are subjected to a searching examination. If he retains his power, it is only to become a devil like Karamazov *père*, a cold autocrat like Mr Merdle, or a usurper like Wotan, whose dramatic meaning is locked in his imminent demise. If he gains our sympathy it is usually by losing his authority, like Mr Bulstrode, and falling helpless into the arms of a pitying female. The nineteenth-century father emerges from his long literary ordeal as the protesting paranoiac described by Strindberg, who is finally imprisoned in a straitjacket and removed from the stage. Only a very superficial reading of nineteenth-century culture can persuade us that the popular caricature of the Victorian father is true to the facts. This was the great period of paternal loneliness – the loneliness so poignantly and pityingly described by Edmund Gosse in *Father and Son*. Freud did not so much 'discover' the Oedipus complex as decree the final catastrophe of fatherhood, as the son opts for the mother and puts an end to the father's power.

History has cast a sour judgement on the maternal utopias. The pursuit of a community of free and equal children has led not only to the intended destruction (the 'withering away') of law, but also to the abolition of all those 'little platoons' in which the true maternal spirit was sequestered. Rebellion led neither to freedom nor to equality, but only to a vast impersonal death machine, for which no one could be held responsible since responsibility had been deliberately done away with. Nevertheless, the 'struggle' against the father continues. His dethroning has not diminished a hostility inspired as much by the fear of assuming his burdens as by contempt for his law. Like other gods that failed, the father is hated more in his weakness than he was hated in his strength. This is evident in public life; but it is more evident still in the realm where woman was once supreme – the home. Man is no longer lifelong guardian of the domestic hearth; he has exchanged the onerous duties of fatherhood for the rights of the nanny-coddled orphan. He can walk out on his wife and family just when he wants; he can have his way with women and disclaim all responsibility for the love he might inspire in them. He enjoys that lawless substitute for freedom which ensures that he and all he touches lies bound in servitude.

Men are not loved for their new-found licence. The feminist call for equality, while seeming like a final demand for the abolition of fatherhood, conceals an even more passionate need for its resurrection. Women expect men to assume the posture of responsibility which is the source of law. For this posture guarantees the only freedom that really matters. Say this, however, and you will find yourself in trouble. The orphaned wolves roam the world in search of a father on whom to vent their rage. Speak in defence of him and, if you are a man, you become him. He is like the hunted priest at Nemi; you easily obtain his crown, but only to lose it, along with everything that made the crown worth while.

IN TANDEM

TIM HILTON

I came late to the business of being a parent and have much to learn before I die. As I write I am forty-nine and my son Daniel Hilton is four (four *and three-quarters*, as he would no doubt say). For some reason I can never remember when he joined the calendar. Other dates in any century, foreign telephone numbers, British Museum and Bodleian press marks: all these present themselves quite shortly after I do something in my mind, but Daniel's birthday in the last week of April eludes me. Make of this what you will. Of course I remember the occasion itself. The lights were much dimmer than I had expected. You would have to paint the scene in matt black and maroon with passages of dull yellow. Also everything was noisy, perhaps tumultuous, and lots of people were there, orderlies or students or something, I don't know. I was obsessed with my wife. The worst noises probably came from me, since I'd signed up for pregnancy classes and had indeed attended the first of them, in which fathers were instructed to sing during labour. 'Pretty little black-eyed Susies' was one of my songs and another was 'Oh her name was Lil, she was a beauty/She lived in a house of ill reputey . . .', taught me many years ago by my own father. The half-mother laughed through her pain and then there was a great ultimate crashing and weeping on all sides as Daniel appeared. Afterwards it was my task to find coins for the pay-phone. 'It's a boy!' Why do grandparents then ask such bloody silly questions about how much my boy weighs? It must be something to do with the NHS.

Alexandra, Daniel's mother, says that I was then mad for a month. Certainly I was not urbane. While something incommunicably tender grew between her and our child I circled round cot and home like a bad bear, seeing off friends, neighbours and other innocent well-wishers. This phase lasted until we left London for Cromer in Norfolk, where we lived for the best part of a year. Off went the family as though on holiday: self, wife (she does the driving), suckling, baby things in quantity, books, the cat in a cardboard box, my best Italian racing bicycle and a typewriter, not that I was to do much writing. Daniel's new home was a tall, empty, decayed lodging house. Everything smelt of damp. I opened the windows and broke some furniture to make a fire. We thought Malkin the cat would like the alleys of a little seaside town but he would not go outside and then, when he did, disappeared.

In Edwardian times Cromer nearly became a fashionable resort. Awkward railway lines and the First World War halted this progress. Today it is a likeable place that seems rather lost or detached, certainly behind the rest of the world. Cromer is noted for crabs. I came to know the crabbing families, all of whose sons were brought up to be fishermen. Our house faced the sea at the top of a steep alley called the Gangway, the route down to the part of the beach where fishing boats and the lifeboat are kept. Sleepless, I would open our shutters at midsummer dawns to see the crabbing people going down to the sea. In twenty minutes they had disappeared, beyond sight in the hazy early horizon.

It's said that the fishermen of this part of the north Norfolk coast incline either to salvationist eschatology or to the bottle, according to their native harbour. In Cromer, I fancy, they take comfort from any source. Crab fishing is a cold and dangerous trade. I was interested because it lay outside my window and I didn't have a lot to do besides the housework. New fathers are warned that they will feel excluded in the first few months of a baby's life. This was no trouble to me. I am a cyclist, so I did about eighty miles a day through East Anglia, zipping through those remote, dead villages that are like the England of forty years ago, and in the evening I went to the Red Lion. An entirely self-indulgent life, all will agree. Then one night in the bar I had a sudden and strange epiphany, a vision of mortality and the sea, of drowning adolescence. The crab fishermen are also the crew of the Cromer lifeboat. For generations they have been brave and daring men – or boys, for the lad who came into the pub was little more than that. His father and brothers were with him, otherwise he might not have been served. He must have left school that summer to follow the family occupation. Barely old enough for beer, just old enough for the waves to take him down.

The blinding knowledge of living and dying generations that came over me was so strong that, there and then, I was a changed man. The unexceptional Red Lion on the cliffs in Cromer, photographs of famous storms and rescues round its walls, made me a father; or, rather, terminated the infancy of my fatherhood. I've come to think that you find what it is to be a parent according to adult rhythms and revelations that have little to do with the growth of a child's personality. Indeed if you found the maturity of your fatherhood only at the same time that your child or children found their own maturity in the world then there would be no delight in the difference between being an adult and being a child. I delight in Daniel, and he in me, precisely because our experience of life is so separated. I shy from those father-and-son pairs (numerous in the sixties and later) who proclaim 'we're much more like brothers, really'. There must be something in brotherhood but I would prefer to have a father or a son. Paternity teaches you more about the ends of life. These matters are often in my mind while Daniel scampers around. Perhaps I brood too much: but who is to say when another person should cease their ruminations? Fatherhood has a public face and a privacy that only the individual can discover. You can point out letters in books, teach a son how to whittle sticks, set up sensible trust funds and attend parent-teacher meetings: the tide will wash over us none the less.

* * *

Back in north London and with Alexandra going to work every day I learned about more immediate matters. As young parents do, we read many books about babies and child development. They all seemed very nice and sensible. How do you get a bit of grit out of baby's eye? With the tip of mummy's tongue. Of course no one suggests that gross old dad should start licking away at his child's cornea. All parenthood seemed to me to be examined from a feminine point of view. So it is in the world beyond books. Women are always advising each other about child care: no man tells another man how to be a father. I also began to wonder about the absence of books that deal with fatherhood *per se*. Could it be, I asked myself, that there are areas of life which we can handle, for good or ill, without any help at all from literature? Hundreds of books are written about fathers by sons or daughters but who can easily name books written by parents about their children, apart from – for instance – the narratives by Arthur Ransome and A. A. Milne that converted family history or entertainment into generally pleasant children's literature? The books I'm looking for cannot be numerous. I can summon only one, the once popular *Antony* (1934) by his father the Earl of Lytton. This is, in a specific way, a conventional work. Perhaps its surprisingly large circulation was owed to that convention. For although Antony died in 1932 his father wrote his son's biography in just the manner of those many memorial volumes (often privately printed) that record promise more than achievement, the youthful horizons of the nation's sons who fell in the Kaiser's war.

To return to my Daniel. We know that all young parents fear that their children may have died during the night. When does this fear end? To this day I wake from frequent dreams in which I protect my son from cliff falls; or even without such dreams to prompt me I go to his room at a dawnish sort of time. Then I am reassured by the gentle heaving of a pile of bears. Blond and tousled, in his pretty pyjamas, he looks like an illustration in a children's book. Can this little boy grow up to become a young man who dies in battle – in only fourteen years' time? I think about this with all the more baffled foreboding because I am of the generation that has not known conflict. My grandfather and father came home from the First and Second World Wars, the elder from the trenches and the younger from the desert, and were changed men, ever afterwards remote from their wives and children. At an equivalent age I was racketing around 1960s London, thoughtless, opinionated and improvident. Daniel Hilton's father would probably have been a bad soldier. On the other hand, those of us who grew up in the sixties may have learned – unwittingly or not – to be flexible and helpful parents. This is one of the advantages of peace.

*   *   *

Changes in the modern world allow me to practise homely and pacific skills. In our family I do the cooking, shopping, and also look after our boy for much of his waking time. Therefore he trails behind me, now that he is not pushed in front of me, from shops to swings to friends and the complex nanny-sharing arrangements that govern our days. Sometimes Daniel and I go to London together but mainly we have a beat: backwards and forwards, once and then twice a day, between the Kentish Town Road and the southern end of Hampstead Heath and South End Green with occasional extensions to, for instance, the children's library attached to Keats House, 'Pete's house', in Daniel's understanding, nowadays closed half the week because of local government cuts; or to the pub or the San Siro café where we breakfast in state, me with the papers and Daniel with a comic, chatting away about things that interest or amuse us.

Nobody can be an interesting parent all the time and when I survey our family life I am despondent about the routine dullness of our patch of urban Britain. You can still see a cobbled mews or two in Kentish Town, the last evidence of the way that horse transport coincided with the railway age, and then there are the Greek-Cypriot food shops, the video stores, our favourite fire station, the thirties Lido at the bottom of Parliament Hill Fields, adventure playgrounds car-sprayed with slogans, Kite Hill and then we're home. On Fridays it was Daniel's treat to come back on the train that does this sort of journey by the North London line. They've changed the rolling stock this year but we knew the last of the old clanking trains. Hand in hand, we always stood at the end of the platform to see the engine driver. One day it was a person who looked both nice and corruptible. A fiver and my boy's dream came true. Yes, Daniel Hilton drove a train from Camden Road station to Hampstead Heath station. Can any other contributor to this book claim such a fatherly enterprise? Unfortunately we were terrified. It was like growing old at the wrong speed. The permanent way lines dashed towards us in the wrong perspective, everything advancing and not diminishing. We were quite shaken when we got down from the cab and Daniel was never inclined to discuss the adventure, though of course we did tell Mum and she was impressed.

* * *

All these things and so many hundreds more are to be lost from my boy's mind. Like everyone else who lives, Daniel will never recall the circumstances of his first years. It seems to be the wisdom of nature that we cannot remember the time when we were most loved and tended, for otherwise we could not be fully adult. A person able to recall childhood before the age of four or five would, I imagine, be a human monster. All loss of this sort of memory must be for the good of succeeding generations. Perhaps failure of recollection in aged people is a sort of balm: they never rail against it, do they? None the less I lament my feeling of fatherhood as an uncomprehending sea, all things swimming from me as I hope to contemplate my own infancy, or my father's, or his loss of memory, or my son's future; especially Daniel's future, which comes to me in a strange form, through a habit of trying to imagine his adolescent self as though I were remembering him as a teenager – winning cycle races, I hope, and meeting complicated dark-eyed girls – when in probability, at that sort of time in the new century, I will be long or shortly dead.

Such moping will not do. Did you know that it was Schopenhauer who first compared memory to a sieve? Trust a latter-day deep thinker to come up with a useless cliché. Now let's think about the more cheerful subject of modern racing cycling. Amongst the social functions of sport is the bonding it produces between fathers and sons. It happens that cycling is an especially father-and-son activity, both as pastime and as competition. Recently I was at an event and was riding with a friend of mine, of my age, and his son. The boy was showing off in the first few miles, as he should, all was sunlight and brilliance as we swooped through the valleys. The dad was basking in it and I saw the love and the pride and the impression of his own youthful self. Active fatherhood is obviously a way in which we try to stop ourselves from ageing. Less obviously, fatherhood depends on self-esteem. I don't think there's anything wrong with this. An estimate of oneself is as important to a prisoner as to a general. But of course I wish there were more in me to be the subject of Daniel's future pride. One day I hope we will ride in the lanes that I knew as a teenager and chat about such things. But this may be a fantasy, and nothing in the look of the world persuades me that in a few years' time any young man will wish to have a conversation with an old man, or at any rate not with me. Meanwhile we're planning to get a childback tandem from a man I know who builds such things. These are reputedly sociable machines, but in fact it's rather difficult to hear what the other rider is saying!

FATHER ISLAND

JULIAN HENRIQUES

Turning a page, an old leaf-speckled specimen, paper yellowed and pitted with browned print like an overripe banana; turning a page with pencil marks in the margin, underlinings, notes, stains and other indecipherable remains; turning a page patterned with decay, eaten by insects and disfigured by the mould of ages; turning a page a slip of paper catches the breeze like a butterfly and tears out from between the leaves. Removed from its mark of several decades it flies off across the veranda on a clear bright tropical morning after the night's rain.

Laying the book on the long arm of the Berbice chair I go to retrieve the scrap of paper from amongst the wet succulent stems at the foot of the terrace. The garden is full of giant glossy versions of the plants that, before my first visit here, I'd only known in pots indoors. Without seasons or twilight the generations of growth and decay are more excessive in the tropics. Life is larger, as if the humid air itself supported the huge flora, like the ocean does whales.

I find the fragment bears my father's hand. It's written in his fountain pen – before a Biro took over his notes. But it's too small a scrap to decipher any words on it. The place it had been keeping all the years was in a nineteenth-century edition I had inherited from his library. The book was one he must have read for his doctoral research on race and class in Port Antonio, down the Portland hills to the sea, where I now sit.

This was where my father had first returned to the Caribbean after leaving as a child and where he had later taken my mother from England. It was also where he had brought his family 'home' on holiday to the Caribbean in the mid-sixties. The journey had been well planned. Dad conveyed the guidebooks, plane timetables and maps down from his study to spread on the kitchen table. (The kitchen walls were already decorated with maps plotted in red and photographs from earlier camping trips across Europe.) He named the fruits whose new tastes we were about to discover: sour sop, sweet sop, starapple, otaheite apple, neeseberry, papaw, passion fruit, honey banana and mango.

From Leeds, where he was a university lecturer, Dad laid out a whole Caribbean of the imagination. For me, my two younger brothers and my mother he traced our proposed route between the islands: Barbados, Grenada, St Vincent, St Lucia and then Jamaica, like a string of pearls. The five of us, not to mention various friends and their children, took up half the seats on the tiny planes that flew the Antilles. Appearing at the last minute my father was always juggling a Scotch, cigarette, his briefcase and the tickets before we squeezed on board. When we reached Jamaica, Dad rented a house amongst scarlet bougainvillaea in the same Portland hills.

A moment reflecting in the quiet of the early morning – turning the pages on the spot from where I could look back to my father's past and forward to my daughter's future. With my family around me – Parminder my wife, our daughter Mala and my mother, Rosamund – I am glad to be treading in my father's footsteps. For me, Port Antonio is a place like a palimpsest: the layers of each generation's return leaving its trace on the next, like the old print penetrating through one page to the next. In fact it had been Rosamund who had organised this 'holiday of a lifetime', as she called it. She had seemed anxious for her granddaughter, though not even two years old, to see Jamaica, not even the island, but Port Antonio in particular. The morning after the London flight Rosamund had only been impatient to leave Kingston for the country.

The house on whose small veranda I am sitting commands a crab-grass-covered hilltop, like a rock in a sea of tropical growth. With the positioning of a great house this holiday retreat, where the water seldom runs in the tap, has the entire vegetable kingdom as its domain. It is remote even from the isolated hamlet that goes by the name of

Nonsuch. All around the bush rises to the Blue Mountains behind on slopes fuelled by the highest rainfall on the island.

In the valley below vast splay-footed trunks support the pillars of trees that rise up to the green roof hung with creepers. Noisy parrot squawks pierce the early morning mists, perhaps remembering the war cries of the Maroon warriors whose descendants still live further up in the mountains. Down the hill hide the 'farms': patches of banana, plaintain and breadfruit trees and the small family plots producing the subsistence ground provisions of yam, dasheen and sweet potato. 'Scratch the ground and anything will grow', but with little hope of commercial profit. Not many of the young people here see any style in farming. This tropical paradise is Jamaica's least developed parish – the poor man's hell. It is also the rich man's heaven, accommodating only the wealthiest of tourists in the most opulent of hotels. One of these can be seen from near the house – a brilliant white wedding cake confectionery castle with countless turrets, crenellations and gables – surreal between green palms, well-watered lawns and the blue of the Caribbean sea.

Turning the page, my mother takes Mala down the precipitous track from the house in her pushchair. In so many ways I want to father her in just the same way as I was fathered. It was a good relationship. There was never anything I could do that my father didn't support and encourage. It had always been like that right through the pot-smoking hippy sixties. I remember so well what must have been the last conversation we had before he went into hospital in 1976, where he died within weeks of cancer. We were walking on the shingle beach at Hove near the power station. He was very frightened, but also philosophical. He told me that the greatest pleasures in his life were what he had been able to share with other people: a view, a taste sensation, an enthusiasm. The communication was all, he said.

Even having brought Mala here, how can I make her grandfather be real to her? How can I ever remember him well enough for her? He died fourteen years before she was born, well before I ever met Parminder. I still want to tell my Dad everything that's happened since he died. I want to remember everything about him. And there are all those little things I want Parminder and Mala both to know . . . he had a way of sitting on his heels on the white Indian carpet at his parties and telling stories to the amusement of the group that inevitably gathered round. He had all the charm in the world. The house was often full with distinguished friends from his sociological research and travels round the world: the Caribbean, France, America, Brazil. He and Rosamund loved to entertain and the food, wine and conversation flowed. As the eldest son I was the one who served the drinks at their summer parties – elegant evening dresses sweeping the lawns of the professor's Sussex home. I will always have an image of him framed by plants in the doorway that led to the garden and his study outside.

After he died my mother made her home the family's, even though her three sons had their wives and children. There was always the Saturday lunch which she provided each week. The meal was a chance to be a child again – basking in his mother's adoration and giving her pleasure simply by eating. After lunch, before rushing on with the weekend, was a little time and space to deny the realities of an adult life brought on by parenthood and parent death. Mothers make this especially easy for boy children.

Here in Jamaica, more than anywhere else, you are your parents' child: 'Oh and your uncle was so and so, you must know my cousin . . . are you related to . . .?' First returns to the island were always about them finding out which family I came from rather than me finding any roots they didn't already know about. My reasons for wanting to return home to visit were the same as theirs for leaving – the smallness of the island where everyone knows everyone else's business.

A little later in the day Rosamund struggles back up the hillside with Mala peacefully asleep in her pushchair. She relates where she's been and who she met in the village and how she must have made such a sight to them, an elderly white woman manoeuvring a little brown child round the pot-holes of Nonsuch's only 'paved' street. 'But,' she said, 'I explained that I was her grandmother and that we'd brought her here to discover her roots.' They all liked that immensely, she added proudly. In fact if the conversation had gone on there would have been quite a lot more explanation, given Mala's Punjabi half from Parminder.

Turning the title page – *Marly; or the Life of a Planter in Jamaica*, Glasgow, 1828 – opposite the frontispiece engraving comes the full description of the book 'comprehending characteristic sketches of the Present State of Society and Manners in the British West Indies'. I wonder if my father had read the book in England, or here like me. By the number of markings it had made quite extensive source material for his own research on the slave-owning plantocracy at the beginning of the nineteenth century. The appeal of the book for me, and I imagine for him, came in part from it being cast as the narrative of a return. Marly, the hero of the tale, set sail from Scotland to reclaim the inheritance of his grandfather's sugar estate appropriated by an unscrupulous executor. It was a young man's adventure.

Secretly I had wanted my daughter to be a boy. Then I could repeat my relationship with my father in a family of boy children as ours had been, to do everything for the first time, a second time. With three sisters Parminder also, despite her feminism, admitted a little pang for the acclaim that only male childbearing brings the traditional Indian household. I wanted my child to do the same things with me as I had done with Dad: boys' things, like fixing plugs and putting up shelves. Only I planned to do them without losing my temper in the way he had often done with me. (Also, I have to admit, I wanted an excuse to build model aeroplanes again.)

When Mala came out a girl we had to think again. From her first cry in this world it was clear that she was not Parminder or me or anyone else but her own person. Sure we could both see ourselves in her, but the strongest spirit was entirely herself, 'a little madam' as she was soon called by her adopted Jamaican grandmother, Vida Menzies. Yet sometimes coming in from work, catching Mala unawares, or in a certain light, she would overpower me as a little mirror image of myself. She looked just like a minute black-and-white snapshot of me crouching on the seat of a cane chair in the conservatory of our Leeds house. As for the household jobs, Mala really likes helping me, selecting the screwdriver, gimlet or pliers and climbing up to hand the correct tool to me at the top of the ladder. I do to her what I loved having done to me, like stroking her forehead at night just to send her to sleep, as my father did.

Already as I write, moments of her childhood have become memories, like the day when she came back from nursery school and wrote her name for the first time. Or our conversations, carrying her to nursery school on my shoulders, again as my father did to me. Or the park festival starting with Gujarati musicians and dancers in procession through the audience led by two men dressed up as horses. It was brilliant sunshine punctuated with the noise of the drums, trumpets and bells. Mala was transfixed by fear and fascination. With eyes wide watching the fantastical horsemen, she clung on to me for dear life. I cried behind my sunglasses, seeing it all for the first time. Mala felt my feelings too. Afterwards she would not let me go even when Parminder wanted to take her.

Turning the page of her sketchbook, my mother is working in the shade with the commitment of someone refinding her first career as an artist after we'd all left home and after her widowhood. She entered everything with the enthusiasm of a teenager fresh to her responsibility and independence. She loved any adventure, especially in wild places, like the tropical surreal forests in Alejo Carpentier's *The Lost Steps*, her favourite book as an art student. It was a thick-stemmed ideal of nature, as painted by Henri Rousseau, that inspired her work. A print of his 'Snake Charmer', vines like vipers, hangs in her bedroom.

Once she told me that she could never have seen herself married to 'a bowler-hatted Englishman'. From her childhood reading, she said, she'd always been fascinated by the jungle. We shared a sense of shape and shade which she sketched and I photographed as colour studies for her next mural. On Christmas Eve we had spent an hour or so discussing its composition and placing to best effect in the hall of Vida and her sister Joyce's home where we were house guests.

Turning the page on the memory of my father in his study. As a child, I always remember the air thick with cigarette smoke, like incense, the tables as altars, covered with brightly striped African rugs – from six months in Ghana just after independence – and piled high with the sacred offerings of books. Entry was by invitation only. My mother insisted we had to respect its peace and quiet for the same reasons she had given up her career as an artist for him and us. She illustrated each chapter head of each of his books for publication, though. Parminder and I are of a more egalitarian generation.

Books played a great part in my childhood. I was not very quick to learn to read but even before I could, large numbers of them – about twenty – became the staple presents for Christmas and birthdays. Part of growing up was persuading him to include some of the titles of my choice in the pile, without offending him. My home remains lined with his library – an insulating heirloom of thousands of millions of words against the cold reality of death. Visitors remark sometimes on whether I could possibly have read them all. The shelves bend under the suffocating weight of all that past.

As a child I must have secretly been jealous of the time he spent away from us in his study. I remember always being suspicious of how anything new could be manufactured out of a raw material which was after all only other books. Perhaps that was the alchemy he performed at the typewriter, to which I would never be initiated. Why did it take so long? Writing books seemed to be more important to him than his children and in retrospect I think he gave each of us, from me the eldest down, slightly less attention. For years he talked about his ship coming home. Not understanding at all, I thought perhaps it might be a reference to Port Antonio. Later he explained that what he was waiting for was the recognition for what he had been writing over the years in his study. Only after he died did I find I could abandon my planned academic career in his footsteps.

Turning the pages of our accounts of our fathers' inheritance, Marly and me. Marly, at the point in the story I am reading, has had to obtain a position as a bookkeeper in order to learn the tools of his future profession as an estate owner. Turning the pages and balancing the books – my father's and his. The columns and calculations measure the exact expenditure that turned the slave labour on the rich land into the immense profits taken by the sugar estate owners. We each have a unique middle vantage point – mine between Mala and her grandfather, Marly's between owner and overseer. From his he could observe the two separate worlds of colonial life: the masked balls and revels of the proprietors, and the conditions and customs of the slave workers.

In fact it was only social conventions that separated these worlds. One of Marly's preoccupations that my father shared was an interest in the numerous and various sexual liaisons between black and white, mostly hidden. Their progeny, however, were not. This gave rise to the whole colour caste system which my father claimed in his book, controversially at the time, still described the concentration of the island's power and wealth in the hands of the lighter-skinned Jamaicans to this day. Marly detailed the nomenclature of the colonial system's obsessions with race and power: 'A Quadroon is the child of a Mulatto mother, by a white father. The child of Quadroon by a white man, is a Mustee. The child of a white man by a Mustee woman is a Mustiphini.' After his first book on Jamaica my father was inspired by the sexual rather than the racial side of these liaisons to write a world history of prostitution, in three volumes.

Not long ago at a publisher's party a well-established poet lurched up to me, a little tipsy, saying what a tremendous man my father was, writing all those books on prostitution: 'he was the first person to do that in the sixties, no one else had even thought of it, and he was a black man'. Whatever he did do my father was certainly a man ahead of his times, or to use one of Vida's favourite terms, he was 'previous'. He was also a contradictory person whose greatest strengths were also his weaknesses, who loved impossible opposites and drank too much.

Closing *Marly*, the four of us drive down the hill to Port Antonio, down the steep track from the house, shouting a greeting into the little cabin that serves as a corner shop, scales hanging in the open of the shuttered window for the one day in the week when a cow is killed; otherwise the only stock is cooking oil, soap, and tins of condensed milk and sardines. On past the cemetery where the cows graze, round the pot-holes, the children on the way to the shop, women with their produce on their heads, men strolling cutlass in hand, the church, the rum shop, the school and the store where dominoes are played at every hour, and set back from the road, the little white-painted house bears the sign 'Nonsuch Post Office'. Further down through the coconut groves cars and motorbikes make occasional appearances round the twists in the road where vistas of the Blue Mountains and Port Antonio appear. Other less fortunate vehicles have been picturesquely sacrificed to the gods of tropical nature, pierced by vibrant new growth sprouting from beneath open bonnet and boot, the *coup de grâce* of a vegetable takeover.

Down further, pieces of cane are crushed on the metal of the road as we pick up speed past Breastworks. Here Marly described a bloody battle between the Maroons and the colonial government of the island. The Maroons were the descendants of escaped slaves who for generations maintained themselves in independent communities in Portland, protected by the forests and ravines of the Blue Mountains. They were the first guerrilla fighters whose speciality was ambush. Nanny was the Maroon's legendary warrior queen who was endowed with the magical power of catching bullets out of the air. She was also said to be capable of catching cannon balls between her buttocks – these she farted back at the colonial enemy, with devastating results.

Then on we sweep into Port Antonio through the swaths of sound from the systems on both sides of the road – each in cacophonous competition with the other. This Christmas holiday the hit tracks are Bobby Brown's 'Don't Be Cruel' and Junior Reed's version of 'One Blood':

You can come from Reema or from Stoney Hill,
One blood, one blood, one blood,
You can come from Birmingham or from London Town,
One blood, one blood, one blood . . .

I get a high from that music. One blood, English and Jamaican, running through my veins and my daughter, English, Jamaican and Indian. Nothing alive is pure. Nothing pure is alive, despite the lies of the dead hand of the Colonial past. We are all mixtures. As Shakespeare would now have Edmund say, 'Gods, stand up for half castes.' My brown skin is the colour of the future everywhere.

We reach the run-down market town, for that is all Port Antonio is today. Once it had been prosperous from banana exports. As in every country town square, the buses stop piled to overflowing inside and on top with sacks of coconuts and green banana stems and the odd bicycle. They pant blue clouds of diesel fumes, ready or recovering from the four-hour journey to Kingston on the other side of the island. Each one is customised with bright paintwork tassels, stencils and designs bearing proudly their name front and rear: 'Deliverance', 'Faith' or 'Fortitude' against the bustle and decay around them.

Port Antonio was our point of departure as well as return. It was here at the turn of the century that my grandfather built up the spice business which gave him the wealth to move to the Jamaican capital and then, in 1919, to London. That must have been quite a trip too. According to my Aunt Pauline they were a party of fifteen or so on the boat to Southampton, what with all the retainers and children. My father was two years old and the youngest of seven. He arrived in England the year my mother was born.

We shop in the cool under the red-painted galvanise of Musgrave market. The higglers, the women-only backbone of the domestic economy, sleep over their produce, already exhausted from their early morning bus ride down from their farms. Sometimes they have to be woken to make a purchase. More lively are the hustling money changers wanting to squeeze dollars from the trickle of tourists who make it to this end of the island. Along the street is the hard dough bakery, which I remembered from a page of my research for an A-level geography project on commercial land use in the town. Little has changed since then, twenty years ago, or even, I imagine, from my father's research, fifty years ago. The town has just been slipping slowly downhill.

One day after the shopping we decide to look for some trace of my grandfather's business. Perhaps the shop is still standing, or perhaps there is a photograph in a local history book in the library. My mother takes the lead with morning coffee with one of the town's oldest families. They were pleased to chat but could offer no information. I try a solicitors' office off the main square, whose clerk behind the grilled counter revealed she had known my father from his research there after the war. By the way she smiled she had obviously not forgotten him. As a young man 'from foreign' my father had clearly made quite 'an impression' on this clerk and I suspect a lot of the other light-skinned young women of the town. He was from England and he was Jamaican and he was highly educated. He was also one of the first black presidents of the Oxford Union. My father always embraced the contradictions of his background – even exploited them. But the elderly, bunned, bespectacled lady – Miss not Mrs, she corrected me – couldn't tell me anything about my father's father's business.

We ate lunch – fried fish, stewed fish or curry goat with rice and peas – at the Atlantis, rum shop on one side and restaurant on the other side of the same zinc roof. Served by twins in less than spotless orange pinafores, it was always that they'd just run out of either beer or soft drink, like the fridge couldn't hold both. The establishment appeared to cater largely for the local police, whose station was across the road. Standing on her chair, Mala made eyes at them on the next table: corpulent officers and the younger ones with their revolvers and red braided belts tight round their thin waists. We told her they would be after her if she didn't finish her lunch.

The library could offer no better guide, though the librarian was keen to discuss the importance of my father's books for his university degree. The town's Chamber of Commerce was the next port of call that we all four made together. Our sixteen-month Mala was as usual tearing round in the office. We waited, although completely without an appointment, under the faded tourist posters and calendars sporting the Chinese names of local 'supermarkets', for a Mrs H. S. Rendle. To our enquiries she was happy to tell us how they were making every effort to revive the local economy since the tourist boats have ceased calling on account of a typhoid scare, the result of a rumour which Mrs Rendle claimed to be unfounded. The difficulty of course was lack of government funds. Then there was Hurricane Gilbert, but no, she was sorry she couldn't help us to find the little girl's great-grandfather's business.

So we had to make do with my father's generation. Here the evidence still stood. We took 'English' tea at the De Montevin Lodge, of all the guest-houses on the promontory the only one of red brick rather than white-painted wood and the only one still keeping up appearances in what had once been the fashionable heart of Port Antonio. Fort George Street ran out to a colonial military installation, now a school, between the two bays of the port on either side. Mala, as usual, felt at home, trotting over the expanses of polished wooden floor and pulling the doilies with their glass ornaments off the occasional tables. This is where my father had stayed when he was here on his research. Then it was not a guest-house but the judge's residence – his brother was the judge.

Over tea in front of the white-painted ironwork of the veranda, we talk. For my mother this trip is a visit to her past in which I quite clearly play my father. In the old days, she told us, presumably from what she'd been told, my father couldn't have been more different from his brother the judge, a beacon of rectitude on an island of the usual colonial corruption. Cyril went on to a knighthood and became the Lord Chief Justice of the island. At the front door of the residence the judge would brook no endearments or tokens. Meanwhile at the back door, my mother told us, my father had a more practical attitude. This allowed him to accept what was offered without ever communicating to the judge from which side of the case at trial it might have come.

Turning the pages on the days in Nonsuch, Mum up first in the morning with her coffee and toast on the veranda, expeditions up to Maroon Town or to the beach then singing her granddaughter to sleep. She liked me to cook – plaintain, callaloo, sweet potato, ackee with red pepper and ginger and fish – as it had always been my father who had cooked for us on holiday, to give her a rest. Over the meals came the stories, the retelling of her previous trips to the Caribbean, and even the reliving of her pregnancy with me, in relation to something that was happening with Mala, inevitably prefaced by 'I know you've heard this before, but Parminder might be interested'. A couple of times she mentioned how she had a very bad allergic reaction to some fruit she had eaten on one Caribbean trip. 'The trouble is, damn it, I can't remember what it is I'm not supposed to eat.'

A few days later my mother suddenly took ill with a stomach complaint. In three days she was dead. It was as though she had known why she had to bring us back. My father had died in England. For my mother it was my father's island of Jamaica.

WHAT SHALL WE DO NOW THAT WE HAVE DONE EVERYTHING?

HUGO WILLIAMS

We met on a staircase at a dance when we were twenty-two – we refused to get out of each other's way – and set up home together two days later. Hermine had come over from Paris for a weekend's mayhem and had thoughtfully left her suitcase at the station in case she needed to live with anyone at short notice. After dinner, we went and got it out. Three weeks later she went home to France to collect her things and say goodbye. It was 1964.

Marriage is easy. You can't believe your luck. Why should anyone want to sign their name to such an obvious bargain? You're tripping over yourself. You throw back your shoulders at the world and step across the threshold into a double place where reasons seem to exist for liking yourself. Miraculous. Beautiful. You can't get enough of it. This is the charm of marriage: to be freed from your old self by becoming half of something else, more favourable. It's easy to see why marriage is so popular: everything you do is a present to yourself. In its purest form it is self-love.

Ah, but the real marriage comes later, when her periods stop. I can't imagine making the decision to start having children, but (mercifully) the decision was taken out of our hands, as it should be. The Pill was around in 1965, but we weren't aware of it. We bought little foaming torpedoes made in Ireland, which stung and (apparently) didn't work. From waking in bliss to my brand new improved world, I would wake in the grip of an idea, an abstraction, an impossibility, a delta of tiny responsibilities spreading like cracks across the ice of my lovely new life. Funny how these packages are addressed to us from different parts of the world: all we have to do is ask a girl to dance and they know just where to deliver them, cash on delivery. How on earth would I get enough money? I didn't have a job. I didn't want a job. I woke up crying as my gay little world turned into this difficult new place where I had to . . . *do* things. I mourned my old present-tense life of poetry and parties and postponements and every day the future got nearer.

A first pregnancy is a truce, an interregnum, a valedictory interlude for the new husband. Like his child, he has nine months in which to grow up.

It wasn't so long ago really, 1966, and yet I was given the impression by St Mary's, Paddington that I was the first father ever to attend the birth of his child. I had a letter from our GP saying I could be present if I wanted to and I put on my tweediest suit and daddyest tie to combat the hospital bureaucracy. I was a knight errant on some ill-defined mission to save his lady, though from what I had only the vaguest idea.

As a father barely out of my teens, I was intoxicated by self-importance. I might not be the star, but I was aware of having a plum part in this traditional drama: prestige without pain. I thought it would be easy for me to turn in a convincing performance without getting too involved. Mine would be a cameo role with a certain amount of glory attached to it by association. I would drink a lot, go unshaved for a day or two, become 'stubbly with goodness'.

For my wife there were no such options available. When a nurse came to shave her there was nothing I could do to save her from defilement. The razor-blade packet had a little blue bird printed on it and we seized on this with relief. Did the NHS have a contract, we asked, with this obscure brand of blunt razor blade? The nurse didn't answer. The blue bird was put away for the scrapbook.

A little while later, when the agony began, Hermine asked me to find one of these inadequate weapons so she could commit suicide. My eyes must have been popping out of my head as I caught my first glimpse of what was really going on here.

'The worst thing was if a nurse came in during a contraction', she wrote afterwards. 'They didn't seem to understand the mental effort one was making. They would start talking inanely, asking me questions, so that I had to blurt out, '*I am having a contraction!*' I didn't want to alienate them, but if I didn't get them to stop they would go on shouting at me and touching my stomach, which became intolerable.'

She had already had one injection, which was supposed to be enough. The Natural Childbirth was supposed to take care of the rest, but it wasn't working. I should have sat tight, but I was still doing everything I was told by Hermine in those days. I ran all over the hospital, looking for a sister who would sign a chit authorising a nurse to open a cabinet and give my wife another jab.

I think of all those wasted evenings practising natural childbirth, my wife and I breathing heavily in and out while raising our right arm and left leg. The idea was to learn to relax your muscles independently so they didn't get tangled up in the 'natural' birth process. The exercises were so excruciatingly boring we invariably ended up asleep.

'The injection came and I remember no more, till half waking in a new room with a new, lesser pain, I thought vaguely that I was on the lavatory and I began crying because I had given birth unknowingly.'

After all the trouble she'd been to, this is what it came to: I was there and she wasn't; I had seen someone coming out of someone and she hadn't. Whether she blames me for this I don't know. I blame myself.

Our daughter, meanwhile, was fast asleep herself, one little hand showing above the bedclothes. Clenched in it was my heart.

* * *

Everyone has their favourite row, the one they do best, the one they feel gets to the heart of the matter. It doesn't, but they think it does at the time and that's what inspires them, what fires their imagination, what cuts them off from the truth. The words may vary with the subject matter (the least important aspect of a row), but the basic format will remain the same: *how dare you!*

A favourite row may become confused with a partner's favourite row over the years, but your own will always be distinguished by that extra sense of commitment, of coming *home*. When people recognise they are in the presence of their very own row, their hearts leap up, they throw back their shoulders at the world, they feel themselves capable of anything. Unfortunately they are.

If they'd had a tape recorder running during some of their rows they would have written something genuinely spontaneous by now. They would have found out what their thoughts sounded like speeded up to the limits of pronounceability. They would have discovered how good their grammar really was, how articulate they remained under pressure. They might not like what they found. If they were unlucky, as I once was, they would find out what they were thinking about the moment before a scream, or a punch. If they were lucky, as I was, they would get a chance to rewrite their row before the general public were invited to give their verdict on it.

So why the pussyfooting? Isn't it obvious?

Rows with my daughter follow the same pattern as rows with her mother, so (I reason) they must have something to do with me. What happens is this. I protest at some minor outrage and instead of mollifying me briefly and changing the subject (easy, but cheap), they up the stakes by leaving the room. Falling for it every time, I run after them, begging forgiveness, fired by the knowledge of my own weakness. It isn't long before money is mentioned by me, along with the difficulty of working at home. After that, it is downhill all the way, with tears (mine) at the bottom.

The row is basically a star vehicle for a time-honoured performance in which I do all the talking (shouting), but my wife or daughter gets the best part and all the notices, being free to react visually, without encumbrance of hackneyed speech. A critic would point out that this row of mine wasn't really a row at all and that that was where it was flawed. I would answer that this was an intrinsic part of its creation, the thing that spurred me on to ever dizzier heights of self-justification.

Families aren't card houses that one wrong breath can bring tumbling down, but at the time you think they are, you imagine it's all over, that you've finally blown this perfect construction of yours. It has been this sensation that all was now lost which has caused me to act without hope on some occasions.

When I think about fatherhood, a single memorable day comes back to haunt me, cutting me off for ever from any comfortable feelings I might have on the subject.

My daughter (fourteen) and I (thirty-seven) were drawing up our troops on the battlefield of the lunch table. There followed an explosion and an exit. I ran after her and, with a solicitude that was really anger, asked what was the matter. She flew at me with fists flying and I slapped her round the top of her head. I wore my watch on my right wrist in those days and as I lashed out the bracelet expanded and the watch hit her in the mouth. Blood began to flow. Moments of horror followed as I realised it was not just her lip that was broken: I had chipped one of her precious front teeth. It occurred to me that one ought to be able to decide against anything so grotesque, in the way that one decides not to poke a pen in one's eye. But no. There it was in my hand, a piece of my daughter's body that would not grow back again.

The horror increased as the three of us sat in a taxi on our way to University College Hospital. There was a bus strike that day and like the blood in our veins the traffic was frozen solid. For one terrible hour we sat murmuring and bleeding into handkerchiefs in the back of that taxi, which seemed to be transporting us gradually to hell.

Does one grow up suddenly at such times, or down? I remember wanting to turn away into the darkness, yet knowing that I had to fumble forward, pretending there was light up ahead, pretending I was still me.

Looking back, the wilderness of our joint adolescence stretches as far as the eye can see, while behind it, obscured by it, the much longer period of childhood seems to have concertinaed inexplicably with only one or two ecstatic moments sticking up from the gathered folds. My daughter's head hovering just behind my own as she perches on my back, head and shoulders above the world, reaching out to touch people's hair at some gallery opening. Her tangled blonde hair flowing in the wind as she races down Parliament Hill on one of her birthday party picnics, ice-cream all over her face.

For a brief period, she spoke poetry. Quickly grasping the new game, she would stand beside my desk, dictating them as fast as I could write. If I look up now, I'll see her outside on the pavement, standing on a chair, selling them to passers-by for 10p each. If I listen, I can hear her on her walkie-talkie, playing 'Star Trek to the Planet of the Apes', which is in the attic with the dressing-up clothes. One person has to stay on base, while the other moves around the house saying 'Beam me up, Scotty'. I remember having to rush back home from somewhere to find the LSD which I'd left lying around, visions of our little darling pinned to the wall by dinosaurs, never again to recognise her Dad, who'd be in prison anyway.

All sense of time passing is lost in the glow of those golden days that I didn't know were golden. Did she have growing pains once, or many times? Did I rub her legs for her, or did I give her an aspirin and tell her to go back to sleep? I know what I'd do now of course, but it is too late. All that is gone and doesn't bear thinking of.

Why do I feel such a helter-skelter of joy and remorse looking back on my family life? When I look at photographs of us then, photo-booth snaps on the way to Paris, off to Brighton, going back to school, I feel a split second of shame at some mysterious deficiency lurking almost visibly in my expression, before pride wells up to mask it. I look again and it is gone. Surely I can't have been faking it all those years?

Fatherhood is a mirror in which we catch glimpses of ourselves as we really are. It seems to me now that I skimped on my daughter's childhood in order to have my own life. You can do that if you only have one child: the parents outnumber it two to one, so the child has to grow up fast and join their gang. Better than no gang at all, I suppose, but it isn't the same as running wild in the country.

If children provide a glimmer of self-knowledge for their parents, does this knowledge include a true perception of their children? What a joke! That clarity is reserved for their perception of us – from their infantile fascination with our absurd noses, to their teenage contempt for our absurd values. Ashamed of my cheapskate life on the dole and grant, my daughter told her friends I was manager of the Waterman's pen factory. I felt no qualms about letting her sleep with her boyfriend in the house, but perhaps she wished I had.

I remember so well opening the front door on her first short sticking-up bleached blonde hairdo, the look of interested defiance on her face as I travelled the million miles from dismay to acceptance, from father to friend.

– What do you think?
– I like it.
– Really?
– Yeah.

And I did like it. I loved it. Or rather I liked something about it, its dandified contempt for what was given. Even as I smothered my sadness for the chestnut mane that had gone, I loved its mad bravado, its air of taking on the world. I looked at her with shocked, admiring eyes, and yet I experienced a sinking feeling, as if a great ship were getting under way, its thousands of streamers lifting and breaking finally as it pulled away from the quay.

Writing about fatherhood I have the impression I am cutting up sentimentality into smaller and smaller parcels in order to disguise its true nature: the dangerous illusion of flesh and blood, that it is part of us. When I saw her new hair, I found myself wanting to say, 'You're just so brilliant you can do anything,' as if I were talking to myself. I had to stop myself, having no way of proving it. In the past, my wishful compliments and reassurances have sometimes overshot the world's opinions and been returned to me with a disappointed look, as if she would rather have found out for herself that she couldn't draw very well, or play darts.

The fact remains that from the moment I first saw her, lying quietly in her first clothes, having a nap after her ordeal, I was convinced of her superior beauty and intelligence. I presume this is the mechanism which tries to persuade us to put our children's needs before our own, which tortures us if we fail to do so, and which finally persuades the child to agree with us and leave home.

Our daughter is grown up now, with a past of her own – as I write she is somewhere in Asia – while we two imagine we are still young, with a future ahead of us. What shall we do next, I wonder, now that we have done everything? I would like to look forward, but it is hard, with the weight of such experience dragging one back. Did these things really happen? Did I really once break my own daughter's front tooth?

I'm afraid so, but there's a happy ending to the story. At the end of a seemingly endless journey across London, the traffic would part, the taxi we were huddled in would reach University College Hospital and a man would stick a little false piece on to my daughter's tooth. Colour would seep back into the world, words would be tried out like very thin ice, we would buy a teddy bear and a duvet in the Reject Shop and by some twist of irony my daughter would thank me. I remember we went to see some terrifying film about violence in a post-holocaust wilderness. Magically, she enjoyed herself. A smile was attempted. A mirror was looked in without undue horror. Tea was made.

I myself had further to go before getting out of that darkened hall, that endless taxi ride, that crowded waiting room. After a year I would cease to think about it every day and start to think about it every other day. Writing about it now may be the last twist of the knife. In a strange way I hope it isn't. When it happened I remember casting around for a pin-hole of light back into the real world where everything was as it should be and I was still good old me. Living now in that familiar world I want to be able to look back through that pin-hole occasionally to a time when such feelings were still alive and tender and I seemed to be carrying something precious and breakable in my arms towards some achievable goal. Sometimes, as now, I manage it for a moment and my scalp tingles again with the old sensation. I suppose it is through such shocks and shake-ups that one learns how unimportant ends are compared to means, that the best we can do is try to stay cool and muddle through.

I gave the offending watch to the TV repair man. I wear my watch on the other wrist now, in memory of that day.

PATRIMONY

MICHAEL HOFMANN

I don't really belong in here, I'm not a father yet, I just have a baby.
It's a kind of intermediate stage. From here, some develop into
fathers, some don't. With me, I feel it's some way off. When
someone asks me how I want to bring up my son – a word that frightens
me – I panic and shrug and say, 'In an old-fashioned way, I suppose.'
I'm just sitting beside a bucket of sand watching a fire. In time, it'll
burn out of control anyway.

Nor – as you see – do I want to write anything continuous. I couldn't.
Something encyclopaedic. A measured aldermanic (aldermaniac?!) stroll
all round the topic, omitting nothing, coming to balanced and important
conclusions. I'm not like that. The subject isn't like that. It's discontin-
uous, unpredictable, spasmodic.

Besides, in the year, just under, of my boy's life, I've noticed a
horrible tendency in myself towards sagacity, even preachiness. I don't
think I was like this before. But having a child is like having access to a
soapbox. It gives you a tiny area of expertise, material, conviction. I
could preach, go up and down with a sandwich board, 'No Peanuts', but
I'd sooner not. You can't preach in ribbons of speech like this. There's
a lovely German proverb about kneading one's bread from crumbs,
lovely because it's so childish to think that bread is made out of crumbs,
and that things can be reversed, un-cooked or un-broken again. But in
fact it can't be done. These are crumbs.

Sitting with my father and son a couple of weeks ago, I had the strange and not unhappy feeling of not existing. My father was paternal – tender and sovereign and irresponsible – my son displayed his waxing playfulness and a touching confidence, they seemed to match up, and I was cancelled out. Gone into a generation no longer – and not yet – of biological significance.

When he's there, M., he's very much there. No one looks at or talks about anything else. (Apparently this is also true of cats.) But when not . . .? It's so peculiar that I haven't undergone physiological changes like his mother. I feel faithless, as though my attachment to him was weak, which it's not. How I wish I felt his absence like a pain.

Because I am – or have been (the perfect tense of fatherhood, the *passé accompli*?!) very close to him. Circumstances fell out so that I held him first, and had to introduce him to his mother. Once he was weaned, it was largely me that fed him. He smiled for me and knew me. I minded him for a few months; if something was the matter I could fix it. I wasn't rivalrous, but I wanted there to be no distinction in his mind between his mother and me, I wanted to inhabit the same niche. At the same time I felt like a confidence man, like the character in Randall Jarrell's poem:

> Reminded of how Lorenz's just-hatched goslings
> Shook off the last remnants of the egg
> And, looking at Lorenz, realized that Lorenz
> Was their mother.

A sudden jolt at a new meaning of things. Dylan singing, 'If I don't make it, you know my baby will.'

Two things, two things only. One. Looking. When he's there – when I'm there – being unable to take my eyes off him, looking for myself I suppose, trying to devour him with my eyes – it can't be done – wanting to catch him, remember his fingers are just so long and no longer, his eyes are just not brown (they are). Looking as denial.

And two. Forgetting. Forgetting he's there. Forgetting all about him. *Christ, what about – !* Of course. Looking as atonement or ransom.

But he forgets too. When you give them back the toy they've dropped on the floor, they apparently think it's something completely new. Their continual surprise and delight. Like a couple with Alzheimer's, our recurrent love at first sight. I come in the door – *Christ!* – while he, he lets a line of dribble go down his chin, as if we were both characters in Genet. (Or are you pleased to see me?!)

He stands up in his cot, arms aloft, like a suitcase waiting to be claimed, wanting to be picked up and swung away.

To myself, I don't feel like someone with a child. I still feel childless, fearful of children, fearful of myself as a demanding and ungrateful child, attitudes I've had for twenty years now, since I was a child myself. My father dinning it into me at an early age that having a family was his big mistake, and that if I was anything like him, I should avoid it myself. I felt no illogic or contradiction as I listened to him. My sense of privilege at being around to hear this actually lent force to his words. I listened sympathetically, sorrowfully, and resolved to do as he'd said, not as he'd done.

Now, though M.'s already almost a year old, it's as though there was still uncertainty about his existence. Not a fact, but a vibration, yes/no, looking and forgetting, wanting to be marked by it, and not wanting anything to show.

The Germans, most (?) unphiloprogenitive of peoples, partly for honourable reasons – the split country (until recently), the perfectionist's fear of the future – partly for dishonourable ones – a cosy, adult and selfish society they are too greedy (and also too uncommitted) to share. Grass, an exception, in his book *Headbirths or The Germans are Dying Out*, contemplating a different, teeming Germany with the population of China. Scary.

So I have a child without being a philosophically committed father. The doubting father. How little this matters – what can doubts do to M., he exists! He proves it thus. How much more important that I, clumsy and impatient, should quite unaccountably prove able to change and dress and feed him.

I feel he exists most strongly when he is independent of me in some tiny way. (My looking at him does nothing to help establish him.) When he lifts his hands to touch the tufts of hair over his ears – how can he have become aware of them?! – or taps at his head with his wooden hammer to test the effect. Then he is agent and acted upon, and I am nowhere.

My mother's (to me) offensively purposive understanding of his activities: everything is geared towards walking or talking or some such goal. I say it is all an end in itself, and pleases me for being that. She talks about his *Feinmotorik* – I reply that he has none.

The extension of feelings and vulnerability towards all of life. I have become visible to such categories as little girls or old women. Pushing a pram and meeting a fellow walking his dog, we acknowledge each other, we are doing comparable things. Stepping outside to bin the rubbish on holiday, and seeing a toad hop away from the light. A pang, a feeling of softness and guilt, as though I had just missed treading on M. A tadpole is relevant, or turtles hatching from their eggs under the sand, and sprinting for their lives into the water, and the many, many that never make it. Soft-shelled too. Where are their fathers?!

His toy. The green baby and mother – must it be? – turtle on a string. Pull them apart, the little one scuttles up to its mother's stomach, whereupon she scuttles off, holding him to her.

Irritation. The seeming pedantry of reclassifying all relationships: that my father and mother are now 'Opa' and 'Oma', my sisters aunts, and I – help – 'Papa'.

Having M. has wrought havoc on my personal pronouns. I am forever making every conceivable kind of mistake with them: gender, number, person. It's as though a number has been added to some small (say, binary) system of numbers, and thrown it into confusion – I once spent weeks dialling my own telephone number without realising it. I even complained to the operator that it was constantly engaged.

His dot-and-carry-one crawl. A crawl that limps. His right knee drawn under him in the correct piston fashion, the left leg merely swings out. The Ministry of Funny Crawls, someone said. His rusty, unfamiliar laugh like a malfunction.

The young John Osborne (why?) quoting Hegel: 'The birth of children is the death of parents.' Not something a parent would say, and, happily, it doesn't feel like it.

As a kind of advertisement for myself, I broke my ban on his watching television so that we could sit through a natural history film together. The subject was the seahorse, and he saw with me a hugely pregnant male seahorse (the seahorse is one of just two or three species where the male carries the eggs and hatches them, and certainly the one that does it with most style, if I remember, the others are types of worm), spilling tiny miniatures of itself out of a hole in its belly. It's like alphabet soup of one variety only, all q's or Greek zetas, beautifully upright (baby seahorses don't crawl), ribbed like a trachea, coming out and straight away drifting into seahorsehood, snapping at minute bits of food, hooking on to seaplants and swaying in currents. Like a car transporter that is itself in the form of a car. The distinctly peculiar sensation when the Cambridge scientist had to help, bunting them out with the tip of her forefinger when they were stuck or breech. But afterwards, what of their sibling relationships? How can they be reunited? How do they know their father (or do they think it's the scientist)?! He's done more for his babies than I for mine, but with less reward.

HEART TO HEART

STEWART BROWN

How should I address you, little one, on the eve of your
    birth?
What can I say that might ease your passage through the
    bloody gates of life?
It is such a short way to travel, the thickness of your
    mother's flesh
out towards the light, and yet the farthest journey you
    will make.
I will be waiting for you; the fat, bald, bearded one,
    looking afraid
and in the way. I will say something conventionally
    clichéd
and probably cry; do not be ashamed of your old dad so
    soon.

This is not what I wanted to say. I wanted to talk to you
    seriously, gravely,
in a way that will not be possible tomorrow. Tonight we
    can speak
of the Mysteries, of the deep truths, of the real meaning of
    things.
Tomorrow it will be all nappies and baby blues. So, how
    to begin?

*I feel I know you quite well already, like prisoners in
    adjoining cells*
*tapping the pipes, we've shaken hands through the womb
    wall,*
*and that brief scan, opening the grille, gave me an image
    to nourish,*

*to flesh out with the features of your tribe. But I
    recognise,*
*of course, that I invent you; I am really talking to
    myself.*
*And that is the ultimate Mystery, the deepest truth, the
    real reason why*
*there is finally nothing to say, except, that I will be
    waiting for you,*
always, *at the school gates, outside the party, at the
    station,*
in your triumphs and your griefs, and later, if there's
    another place,
*I'll be the fat, bald, bearded one, looking afraid and in the
    way.*

TINY FEARS

JOCELYN TARGETT

I'm expecting my first baby, and I think of nothing but the terrific times I've got in store – the giggling, the cuddling, the running around, the spitwashes, the Christmases, the sulks, the quick hot breaths and sunshiny grins of this chubby bundle, half me, half the woman I love. I drift by baby shops and find myself gawping at all the little things. I turn the pages of baby books and tickle the chins of the cute pictures. I look at pushchaired couples and yearn. Today I caught sight of my boss at work, slipping a photo of his two-year-old from his wallet and cherishing her: that'll be me soon, I think, and I smile warmly to myself.

But there are fears. Not for my baby – I am a born optimist and am convinced down to my DNA that Sweetie will be sane, healthy, bright and charming. No, the fears are mostly for myself.

On the face of it, they are rather tame fears, slight and internal – nothing in any way grotesque or life threatening about them. Still, people get scared by the oddest things – one man's pet is another's panic – and, though tiny, these are the darkest, wildest, grisliest fears I have.

I am in a horror-flick of their making. Some nights, they wake me with a start, my eyes staring. When I look in a mirror, there they are, looming behind me. I am, you see, a paternophobe. I fear what is now incontrovertible: I can't wait to have a baby, but I am scared of turning into a father. Actually, that's not quite exact. What I'm really scared of is turning into *my* father.

And of course, that's already begun. I bought my first power drill the other day. It was something I'd never thought about until it happened, down at Do-It-All one Sunday evening. I found it an oddly moving experience.

Once, there was a life where drilling was never contemplated and buying a power drill held no fears. Then, recently, there were curtain rails to put up. I found I had need of a drill. Simple! Borrow dad's.

Then there were other things – lights to fit, shelves to fix, little things which, when lumped together, meant one appallingly significant thing: I could use my father's power drill no more. It was time to have my own. That's when I went to the homecare centre and, between the rails of soft-haired rollers and racks of screws and tacks, I aged, as if one more thread connecting me to my own childhood had twisted and snapped, as if youth was a wiggly tooth.

So nowadays I spend happy weekends drilling. I drill holes in the bathroom wall and hang baskets of flowers, holes in the hall and put up coat-hooks, holes in the roof and mend drainpipes. As a teenager, I remember my father D-I-Y-ing as he listened to 'Just a Minute' crackling on the radio. He always had the volume right up, so even when he was knocking, scraping and drilling, he could hear every wheeze and chuckle of what was to me a dated and incomprehensible game. How I hated it all!

Yet I am now him. I even like 'Just a Minute'.

I'm trying to put it all down to what the books call 'the nesting instinct', which will soon pass once the baby's born, leaving Saturdays for the TV racing again. This is a sad delusion: once an eye has been trained to see the little jobs that need doing, it sees them nearly everywhere. Over the decades to come, I'll probably see as much of my power drill as I will of my child. I have moved out of the age of leisure and into the time to be handy. It is as upsetting a development as puberty, except all the spots are on the inside.

*　*　*

Increasingly, I take for granted the terrible truth that all fathers-to-be must bear: that I'm willingly bringing into the world a person who'll grow up to be ashamed of me, embarrassed by me, sorry for me, a person who'd rather I wasn't around, who'll badmouth me behind my back, a person who, basically, won't want to be with me, as if there weren't enough of those already. There isn't a human being alive who isn't thoroughly fed up with their dad's oafish sense of humour, nor one who would happily hang out at parties with the old man for any length of time. I remember, when I was a boy, standing on a stool and massaging suntan lotion across my father's back: it shames me now, but I remember feeling not affection but distaste. One day, I know, my little sweet cub, my child whom I'll love uniquely, will think that way about me too.

People go to the grave regretting being hostile to their parents – but being hostile to parents is an inevitable fact of human life. Children always grow up blaming their parents for something. My parents didn't put a foot wrong in bringing me up – there was nothing to complain about, so I used to say that they'd afforded me too much love and pride and care and that they'd therefore denied me my adolescent's right to a meaningful rebellion against parental tyranny – an absurd gripe, but the best I could think of. Now I realise that it was simply a reflex emotion, something I had to go through. I realise, too, that my children will one day feel the same way about me as they struggle to pull the teeth of their own childhood. But I don't want my babies to feel guilty for the tetchiness they are sure to inflict on me. I promise not to be hurt by it.

* * *

None of my friends are having babies. That's not quite exact, either: *all* my friends are having babies – the friends that aren't I've quickly drifted away from, and I now have new friends, met at antenatal classes, or else people who, once we'd discovered we had pregnancy in common, I've become close to in a confederacy of fear. My girlfriend (we're not married) is five years older than me and she has many dear friends with toddlers who are doing their bit to ease her into parenthood. But my best friend – whom I first knew as a bold, earnest, gauche young man – heard me tell my joyous news and winced. He regards me, I think, as a foolish pioneer, and worries only about the late movies I will no longer be able to see, babysitters being beyond his imagination. My unborn child has distanced me from him; but if he ever has a baby, I imagine it will be the children who return us to one another.

That metallic anxiety of the young and ambitious will be lost to me by then. A pregnancy confirms that the striven for – will I ever fall in love? will I ever have a child? – is beginning to be matched by the attained. I'm told by the woman in the sandwich bar that time lags behind during pregnancy, then flies once the child is born. Well, I don't want time to fly. I have a tremendous, tear-stained longing for my Sweet Baby, but I'm fearful of how I shall cope with the repleteness and the completeness of life after achievement, with the lack of urgencies, with the slackening of convictions, with the slippage of me.

Will I be sad if my baby costs me some of my aspirations? I think I will, and I think Baby is bound to. Having a child, I'm sure, presents the ambitious parent with a few inequitable would-you-rathers: would I rather work late or feed the tot leads ultimately to, would I rather achieve greatness or be loved overwhelmingly by my child for ever more, and I'd choose the love of my baby every time . . . but not without in some sense disappearing as a human being in my own right. He who is not busy being born is busy dying. I am not dying, but a young and selfish part of me is, and I will mourn it when it goes.

PRAYER

ALAN JENKINS

For my unborn daughter
who was not conceived
on a hillside
in Worcestershire,
scratchy with branches
and thickly unleaved,
that seemed sheer
to the giggling pair
who would bump and grind
and backslide
till one or the other
or kingdom come;
or in a punt
lightly moored
and moving lightly
side to side,
hand on heart
and cock in cunt
at a bend in the river
near Cookham, or Cobham,
where willows droop over
and undercurrents wind
together and apart,

a braided rope of water;
or in a single bed
in a poster-hung room
in Brighton or Hove,
in Eccleston Square,
a hotel in Luton
or on a futon
somewhere in . . . somewhere,
not in Belsize Park,
not in a dark
starlit room in W.11;
whose not-mother
did not lie back and say,
with a map of heaven
winking on the ceiling
in Muswell Hill,
Once more with feeling
or curl into sleep
without a word
and smile at the leap
in her womb,
deeply stirred;
not in Ladbroke Grove,
Stretton, Stourhead
or on West 11th Street;
who did not stain a sheet
in Athens, Montpellier,
Amalfi, Rome,
drop into sand
on Ohrid's lake-shore,
drip from a hand
in Toronto and Arles,
smear a pale thigh
in Venice, slick the skin
of Not inside me *in*
a village near Seville
or pearl a chin
behind Marseille St-Charles;
who has not made news

PRAYER

in any Births & Deaths,
whose first breaths
I did not witness
weeping for joy
scared shitless
in the maternity ward
of St Mary's, Paddington
where I did not pray,
silently, Let it be a boy;
who did not come home
in a frilled carry-cot
to a well-appointed mews
called the Winter Palace;
who is not my Alice,
my Lolita, my store
of everything, my –
who is not;
may she never
walk in the way
of deception,
ignorance, fear
earthquakes, avalanches,
flood or fire,
'domestic violence',
the smiler with the knife
the hands at the throat
the panted threat,
the cold self-accuser
the dead-head, the jerk
the jumpy loser
and his See you later
the bullying Gauleiter
the groper at work;
may she not suffer in silence
the stupid taunts
of older girls, then younger
or her lover's wife;
may she not lose
life, love, whatever

is in her keeping
with the freedom to choose;
may she not know hunger;
may she not, daily, nightly
be angry or bored;
may she not live alone,
solitude grown
round her shambles
of a house
with brambles
and lichened stone,
her familiars
a flea-bitten cat,
a blind rat, a mouse –
all four sleeping
in moth-eaten furs –
unless that
is what she wants

AUTHORS' BIOGRAPHIES

JOHN AGARD was born and educated in Guyana and moved to Britain in 1977. Winner of the 1982 Cuba de las Americas poetry prize, two of his collections, *Mangoes and Bullets* and *Lovelines For a Goat-Born Lady* were published by Serpent's Tail in 1990. He has also written several children's books. He lives in Sussex with the poet Grace Nichols and their two-year-old daughter. He has been described by Michael Horovitz as 'an outstanding luminary of the suddenly exploding galaxy of West Indian British troubadores'.

ALAN BRIEN, critic, columnist, humorist, foreign correspondent, now novelist, was born in Sunderland, served as RAF airgunner during the last war, graduated in Eng. Lit. at Oxford. He covered Russia, Vietnam and Belfast, for the *Sunday Times*; New York for the *Evening Standard*. He wrote a weekly essay for the *Spectator*, then the *New Statesman*, over a decade; political comment for the *Sunday Mirror*; social comment for the *Daily Mail*; TV criticism for the *Observer*; drama for the *Sunday Telegraph*; TV, books and film for the *Sunday Times*. For two years in succession he won the 'Critic of the Year' IPC awards. Married for the third time, he and his wife, Jill Tweedie, share eight children.

STEWART BROWN was born in Southampton in 1951 and is currently a lecturer in African and Caribbean literature at the Centre of West African Studies, University of Birmingham. He previously taught in schools and colleges in Nigeria, the Caribbean and across the UK. He has published two collections of poetry, *Zinder* (1986) and *Lugard's Bridge* (1989), both by Seren Books. He has edited several anthologies of Caribbean writing, most recently the collection of short stories *Caribbean New Wave* (Heinemann, 1990) and, with Ian McDonald, *The Heinemann Book of Caribbean Verse* (1992). He has also edited a collection of critical essays, *The Art of Derek Walcott* (Seren Books, 1991) and produced *Writers From Africa*, an introductory guide to African writing (Book Trust, 1990). He is married, with two children, Douglas and Ceridwen – to whom the sequence 'Splashes from the Cauldron', from which 'Heart to Heart' is taken, is dedicated.

OWEN DUDLEY EDWARDS was born in Dublin in 1938, where his father, Robert, became Professor of Modern Irish History at University College, and his mother, Sile Ní Shúilleabháin, was a Gaelic scholar and folklorist. He studied in Dublin and at the Johns Hopkins University, and taught at the Universities of Oregon, Aberdeen and Edinburgh, at which last he is Reader in History. He married Barbara Balbirnie ('Bonnie') Lee of Philadelphia, in 1966: her critical reading of this essay has saved it from at least some errors and infelicities, but she is not responsible for its opinions. They have three children, one a Dominican nun, one a folklorist of literature, one a geologist man of property. Owen Dudley Edwards's most recent books are *Macaulay, Éamon de Valera, The Fireworks of Oscar Wilde*, and *City of a Thousand Worlds: Edinburgh in Festival*.

LAURIE FLYNN was a reporter and producer on Granada Television's *World in Action* programme for eleven years and now works as an independent. He is the author of *Studded with Diamonds and Paved with Gold: Mining Companies and Human Rights in Southern Africa*, published in 1992 by Bloomsbury.

JULIAN HENRIQUES is a film maker and writer who was born in Leeds, Yorkshire, son of the late Professor Fernando Henriques. He has worked and travelled in India, Latin America and the Caribbean. He is married to the film producer Parminder Vir and they live in London with their daughter Mala (b. 1988). His work includes features for *New Society*, founding and editing the journal *Ideology & Consciousness* in the mid seventies, and he was joint author of *Changing the Subject* (1984). He has worked for London Weekend Television and for the BBC where he made films for Arena and Omnibus, and now his own independent company, Formation Films, for Channel Four. *We the Ragamuffin*, a musical set in Peckham, is the latest film he has directed, to be broadcast by Channel Four in 1992.

TIM HILTON is married to the publisher Alexandra Pringle. He is the art critic of the *Guardian*, a writer on cycling, the organiser of many exhibitions and the author of books on Picasso and Ruskin.

MICHAEL HOFMANN was born in 1957 in Freiburg, and lives in London with Caroline Oulton, a BBC producer, and their son Max. He is a freelance writer, reviewer and translator from the German. Among his translations are books by Joseph Roth, Beat Sterchi and Wim Wenders. Most recently, he has translated Wolfgang Koeppen's novel *Death in Rome*. He has published two books of poems, *Nights in the Iron Hotel* (1983) and *Acrimony* (1986), a book in which he laid bare his vexed relationship with his father, the German writer Gert Hofmann.

ALAN JENKINS was born in 1955, in London, where, apart from four years at the University of Sussex and a year in France, he has lived ever since. He is Deputy Editor of the *Times Literary Supplement* and has published two books of poems, *In the Hot-house* (1988) and *Greenheart* (1990), both with Chatto and Windus. He is unmarried.

MERVYN JONES is the author of twenty-three novels, including *Holding On* (a 1975 television series), *Today the Struggle*, and most recently *That Year in Paris*, published in 1988. He has also written *Chances*, his autobiography, *A Radical Life*, a biography of Megan Lloyd George, and is at present working on a biography of Michael Food. Now a widower, he is the survivor of a long and happy marriage, the father of three children, and the grandfather of six.

GABRIEL JOSIPOVICI was born in Nice in 1940 of Russo-Italian, Romano-Levantine parents. He lived in Egypt from 1945 to 1956, when he came to this country. He read English at St Edmund Hall, Oxford and in 1963 began teaching at the University of Sussex where he is now part-time Professor of English in the School of European Studies. He has published eight novels, two volumes of stories, five critical books and his plays have been performed in London and Edinburgh and by the BBC.

LES MURRAY lives in the country 200 miles north of Sydney in Australia. He is father of five children and ten collections of poems. His *Collected Poems* is published in Britain by Carcanet.

NOAH RICHLER is one of five children. He was born in Canada but brought up in Britain, and returned to Canada in his early teens. After studying at Montreal's McGill University and then at Oxford, he settled in London. He has written for newspapers and magazines in Britain and in Canada, but works primarily as a producer of features and documentaries for BBC Radios 3 and 4.

ROGER SCRUTON is a writer and philosopher, based in London, but currently teaching at the University of Boston, Massachusetts. His most recent books are the novel *Francesca* and a collection of stories, *A Dove Descending*, both published by Sinclair-Stevenson in 1991. His *Xanthippic Dialogues*, in which the truth about Plato, politics and erotic love is revealed by the women of Athens, will be published in 1993, also by Sinclair-Stevenson.

JOCELYN TARGETT is the arts editor of the *Guardian*. In 1989 he won the Young Journalist of the Year award. He lives with the journalist, Judy Rumbold. They had a daughter, called Lola, on 17 April 1992.

HUGO WILLIAMS was born in 1942 into a theatrical family. His first book of poems and a travel book, *All the Time in the World*, were published in 1965, the year he married the author and performer Hermine Demoriane. He worked on *The London Magazine* in the 1960s and *The New Review* in the 1970s. His American travels, *No Particular Place to Go*, came out in 1980. He was TV critic for the *New Statesman* and is still their poetry editor. He was theatre critic for the ill-fated *Sunday Correspondent* and currently writes a regular column for the *Times Literary Supplement*. His *Selected Poems* was published in 1989. He lives in London.